Also by Lee Iacocca

Iacocca: An Autobiography
Talking Straight

WHERE HAVE ALL THE LEADERS GONE?

LEE IACOCCA

WITH CATHERINE WHITNEY

SCRIBNER

NEW YORK   LONDON   TORONTO   SYDNEY

SCRIBNER
A Division of Simon & Schuster, Inc.
1230 Avenue of the Americas
New York, NY 10020

First Scribner hardcover edition April 2007

SCRIBNER and design are trademarks of Macmillan Library Reference USA, Inc.,
used under license by Simon & Schuster, the publisher of this work.

For information about special discounts for bulk purchases,
please contact Simon & Schuster Special Sales:
1-800-456-6798 or business@simonandschuster.com

Text set in Electra

Manufactured in the United States of America

1   3   5   7   9   10   8   6   4   2

Library of Congress Control Number: 2007005179

ISBN-13: 978-1-4165-3247-7
ISBN-10: 1-4165-3247-1

For my grandchildren

CONTENTS

ACKNOWLEDGMENTS

Life is a team effort. No one gets very far alone. I have been blessed with an especially large and dedicated group of people who have supported, encouraged, inspired, and challenged me—beginning with my family.

My daughters Kathi and Lia have meant everything to me. My greatest joy is spending time with them and their families— my sons-in-law Ned and Victor, and my seven wonderful grandchildren, who keep me young.

My sister Delma remains my closest link to my roots in Pennsylvania. She holds a special place as the only living person who has known me since I was born.

My companion and confidant, Juliette, has brought me contentment at this stage of my life that I wasn't sure I would experience again.

I am grateful to all the people who support me every day, beginning with my assistant, Norma Saken. Norma juggles the constant flood of information and requests that come through my office, and she is always looking for new projects. I keep telling her, "Norma, I'm supposed to be *retired*," but she doesn't listen.

I also appreciate the efforts of Ken Anderson and Ginny King at Quintile Management, who keep me in business; and Rosa, Raquel, and Elmer, who make my home life easier.

The best part of life these days is my ability to make a difference in the world, and to give something back. Some very talented and devoted people help me do that. Dana Ball along with Lou Lataif and Desi Heathwood work tirelessly at the Iacocca Foundation in order to make my dream of finding a cure for diabetes come true.

My partners at the Iacocca Institute at Lehigh University, and especially Dick Brandt, have created an environment where students from around the world can discover common ground. They are literally changing the world one young mind at a time.

Blake Roney, Truman Hunt, and Brent Goddard at NuSkin, have been an inspiration in their efforts to feed the world's hungry, and have demonstrated that you can do well in business by doing good. I am pleased to be a part of that effort.

Steve Briganti and the hardworking people at the Statue of Liberty—Ellis Island Foundation have provided a constant reminder of the greatness of America, and the role we all have to play.

I am also grateful to my friends in Detroit who keep me involved in the car business, my friends in Washington who remind me how important leadership is, and my friends in California who help me stay engaged and up-to-date in this fast-paced world. And of course, still on my best friends list are Bill Fugazy, Vic Damone, and Nasser Kazeminy.

Finally, I want to thank the people who helped make this book happen. When Jack Romanos, the president and CEO of Simon & Schuster, Inc., approached me with the idea of writing a book about leadership, I couldn't refuse. Jack and I go way back to 1984, when he convinced me that people really wanted to hear what a car guy had to say. The result of that collaboration was *Iacocca*. It has been my privilege to work with Jack again, along with his top-notch team from Scribner/Simon & Schuster. My editor, Colin Harrison, not only kept my language clean and clear, but he also pushed me to go deeper into my thinking about the critical issues of the day.

The Simon & Schuster and Scribner executives Carolyn Reidy, Susan Moldow, and Rosalind Lippel have been enthusiastically behind this project from the start. And, of course, I appreciate the hard work and skill of my collaborator, Catherine Whitney, who was patient and energetic through numerous drafts, and who helped me turn my most deeply felt ideas and beliefs into words people could understand.

Not a day goes by that some perfect stranger doesn't write, call, or approach me in public to talk about something that matters to him or her. The connection I've made with people from all walks of life has been a great source of energy and satisfaction for me. With this book I hope to use that connection to spark an American renewal. Together, we can do whatever we can dream.

PART ONE

WHERE HAVE ALL THE LEADERS GONE?

I

Had enough?

Am I the only guy in this country who's fed up with what's happening? Where the hell is our outrage? We should be screaming bloody murder. We've got a gang of clueless bozos steering our ship of state right over a cliff, we've got corporate gangsters stealing us blind, and we can't even clean up after a hurricane much less build a hybrid car. But instead of getting mad, everyone sits around and nods their heads when the politicians say, "Stay the course."

Stay the course? You've got to be kidding. This is *America,* not the damned *Titanic.* I'll give you a sound bite: *Throw the bums out!*

You might think I'm getting senile, that I've gone off my rocker, and maybe I have. But someone has to speak up. I hardly recognize this country anymore. The President of the United States is given a free pass to ignore the Constitution, tap our phones, and lead us to war on a pack of lies. Congress responds to record deficits by passing a huge tax cut for the wealthy (thanks, but I don't need it). The most famous business leaders are not the innovators but the guys in handcuffs. While we're fiddling in Iraq, the Middle East is burning and nobody seems to know what to do. And the press is waving pom-poms instead of asking hard questions. That's not the promise of America my parents and yours traveled across the ocean for. I've had enough. How about you?

I'll go a step further. You can't call yourself a patriot if you're *not* outraged. This is a fight I'm ready and willing to have.

My friends tell me to calm down. They say, "Lee, you're eighty-two years old. Leave the rage to the young people." I'd love to—as soon as I can pry them away from their iPods for five seconds and get them to pay attention. I'm going to speak up because it's my patriotic duty. I think people will listen to me. They say I have a reputation as a straight shooter. So I'll tell you how I see it, and it's not pretty, but at least it's real. I'm hoping to strike a nerve in those young folks who say they don't vote because they don't trust politicians to represent their interests. Hey, America, wake up. These guys work for *us*.

WHO ARE THESE GUYS, ANYWAY?

Why are we in this mess? How did we end up with this crowd in Washington? Well, we voted for them—or at least some of us did. But I'll tell you what we *didn't* do. We didn't agree to suspend the Constitution. We didn't agree to stop asking questions or demanding answers. Some of us are sick and tired of people who call free speech treason. Where I come from that's a dictatorship, not a democracy.

And don't tell me it's all the fault of right-wing Republicans or liberal Democrats. That's an intellectually lazy argument, and it's part of the reason we're in this stew. We're not just a nation of *factions*. We're a *people*. We share common principles and ideals. And we rise and fall together.

Where are the voices of leaders who can inspire us to action and make us stand taller? What happened to the strong and resolute party of Lincoln? What happened to the courageous, populist party of FDR and Truman? There was a time in this country when the voices of great leaders lifted us up and made us want to do better. Where have all the leaders gone?

THE TEST OF A LEADER

I've never been Commander in Chief, but I've been a CEO. I understand a few things about leadership at the top. I've figured out nine points—not ten (I don't want people accusing me of thinking I'm Moses). I call them the "Nine Cs of Leadership." They're not fancy or complicated. Just clear, obvious qualities that every true leader should have. We should look at how the current administration stacks up. Like it or not, this crew is going to be around until January 2009. Maybe we can learn something before we go to the polls in 2008. Then let's be sure we use the leadership test to screen the candidates who say they want to run the country. It's up to us to choose wisely.

So, here's my C list:

A leader has to show **CURIOSITY**. He has to listen to people outside of the "Yes, sir" crowd in his inner circle. He has to read voraciously, because the world is a big, complicated place. George W. Bush brags about never reading a newspaper. "I just scan the headlines," he says. Am I hearing this right? He's the President of the United States and he never reads a newspaper? Thomas Jefferson once said, "Were it left to me to decide whether we should have a government without newspapers, or newspapers without a government, I should not hesitate for a moment to prefer the latter." Bush disagrees. As long as he gets his daily hour in the gym, with Fox News piped through the sound system, he's ready to go.

If a leader never steps outside his comfort zone to hear different ideas, he grows stale. If he doesn't put his beliefs to the test, how does he know he's right? The inability to listen is a form of arrogance. It means either you think you already know it all, or you just don't care. Before the 2006 election, George Bush made a big point of saying he didn't listen to the polls. Yeah, that's what they all say when the polls stink. But maybe he *should* have listened, because 70 percent of the people were saying he was on the wrong track. It took a "thumping" on election day to wake him up, but even then you got the feeling he wasn't listening so much as he was calculating how to do a better job of convincing everyone he was right.

A leader has to be **CREATIVE**, go out on a limb, be willing to try something different. You know, *think outside the box.* George Bush prides himself on never changing, even as the world around him is spinning out of control. God forbid someone should accuse him of flip-flopping. There's a disturbingly messianic fervor to his certainty. Senator Joe Biden recalled a conversation he had with Bush a few months after our troops marched into Baghdad. Joe was in the Oval Office outlining his concerns to the President—the explosive mix of Shiite and Sunni, the disbanded Iraqi army, the problems securing the oil fields. "The President was *serene*," Joe recalled. "He told me he was sure that we were on the right course and that all would be well. 'Mr. President,' I finally said, 'how can you be so sure when you don't yet know all the facts?'" Bush then reached over and put a steadying hand on Joe's shoulder. "My instincts," he said. "My instincts." Joe was flabbergasted. He told Bush, "Mr. President, your instincts aren't good enough." Joe Biden sure didn't think the matter was settled. And, as we all know now, it *wasn't*.

Leadership is all about managing change—whether you're leading a company or leading a country. Things change, and you get creative. You adapt. Maybe Bush was absent the day they covered that at Harvard Business School.

A leader has to **COMMUNICATE**. I'm not talking about running off at the mouth or spouting sound bites. I'm talking about facing reality and telling the truth. Nobody in the current administration seems to know how to talk straight anymore. Instead, they spend most of their time trying to convince us that things are not really as bad as they seem. I don't know if it's denial or dishonesty, but it can start to drive you crazy after a while. Communication has to start with telling the truth, even when it's painful. The war in Iraq has been, among other things, a grand failure of communication. Bush is like the boy who *didn't* cry wolf when the wolf was at the door. After years of being told that all is well, even as the casualties and chaos mount, we've stopped listening to him.

A leader has to be a person of **CHARACTER.** That means knowing the difference between right and wrong and having the guts to do the right thing. Abraham Lincoln once said, "If you want to test a man's character, give him power." George Bush has a lot of power. What does it say about his character? Bush has shown a willingness to take bold action on the world stage because he has the *power,* but he shows little regard for the grievous consequences. He has sent our troops (not to mention hundreds of thousands of innocent Iraqi citizens) to their deaths—for what? To build our oil reserves? To avenge his daddy because Saddam Hussein once tried to have him killed? To show his daddy he's tougher? The motivations behind the war in Iraq are questionable, and the execution of the war has been a disaster. A man of character does not ask a single soldier to die for a failed policy.

A leader must have **COURAGE.** I'm talking about *balls.* (That even goes for female leaders.) Swagger isn't courage. Tough talk isn't courage. George Bush comes from a blue-blooded Connecticut family, but he likes to talk like a cowboy. You know, *My gun is bigger than your gun.* Courage in the twenty-first century doesn't mean posturing and bravado. Courage is a commitment to sit down at the negotiating table and *talk.*

If you're a politician, courage means taking a position even when you know it will cost you votes. Bush can't even make a public appearance unless the audience has been hand-picked and sanitized. He did a series of so-called town hall meetings last year, in auditoriums packed with his most devoted fans. The questions were all softballs.

To be a leader you've got to have **CONVICTION**—a fire in your belly. You've got to have passion. You've got to really want to get something done. How do you measure fire in the belly? Bush has set the all-time record for number of vacation days taken by a U.S. President—four hundred and counting. He'd rather clear brush on his ranch than immerse himself in the business of governing. He even told an interviewer that the high point of his presidency so far was catching a seven-and-a-half-pound perch in his hand-stocked lake.

It's no better on Capitol Hill. Congress was in session only ninety-seven days in 2006. That's eleven days less than the record set in 1948, when President Harry Truman coined the term *do-nothing Congress*. Most people would expect to be fired if they worked so little and had nothing to show for it. But Congress managed to find the time to vote itself a raise. Now, *that's* not leadership.

A leader should have **CHARISMA.** I'm not talking about being flashy. Charisma is the quality that makes people want to follow you. It's the ability to *inspire*. People follow a leader because they *trust* him. That's my definition of charisma. Maybe George Bush is a great guy to hang out with at a barbecue or a ball game. But put him at a global summit where the future of our planet is at stake, and he doesn't look very presidential. Those frat-boy pranks and the kidding around he enjoys so much don't go over that well with world leaders. Just ask German Chancellor Angela Merkel, who received an unwelcome shoulder massage from our President at a G-8 Summit. When he came up behind her and started squeezing, I thought she was going to go right through the roof.

A leader has to be **COMPETENT**. That seems obvious, doesn't it? You've got to know what you're doing. More important than that, you've got to surround yourself with people who know what *they*'re doing. Bush brags about being our first MBA President. Does that make him competent? Well, let's see. Thanks to our first MBA President, we've got the largest deficit in history, Social Security is on life support, and we've run up a half-a-trillion-dollar price tag (so far) in Iraq. And that's just for starters. A leader has to be a problem solver, and the biggest problems we face as a nation seem to be on the back burner.

You can't be a leader if you don't have **COMMON SENSE**. I call this Charlie Beacham's rule. When I was a young guy just starting out in the car business, one of my first jobs was as Ford's zone manager in Wilkes-Barre, Pennsylvania. My boss was a guy named Charlie Beacham, who was the East Coast regional manager. Charlie was a big Southerner, with a warm drawl, a huge smile, and a core of steel. Charlie used to tell me, "Remember, Lee, the only thing you've got going for you as a human being is your ability to reason and your common sense. If you don't know a dip of horseshit from a dip of vanilla ice cream, you'll never make it." George Bush doesn't have common sense. He just has a lot of sound bites. You know—Mr.-*they'll-welcome-us-as-liberators-no-child-left-behind-heck-of-a-job-Brownie-mission-accomplished* Bush.

Former President Bill Clinton once said, "I grew up in an alcoholic home. I spent half my childhood trying to get into the reality-based world—and I *like* it here."

I think our current President should visit the real world once in a while.

THE BIGGEST C IS CRISIS

Leaders are made, not born. Leadership is forged in times of crisis. It's easy to sit there with your feet up on the desk and talk theory. Or send someone else's kids off to war when you've never seen a battlefield yourself. It's another thing to lead when your world comes tumbling down.

On September 11, 2001, we needed a strong leader more than any other time in our history. We needed a steady hand to guide us out of the ashes. Where was George Bush? He was reading a story about a pet goat to kids in Florida when he heard about the attacks. He kept sitting there for twenty minutes with a baffled look on his face. It's all on tape. You can see it for yourself. Then, instead of taking the quickest route back to Washington and immediately going on the air to reassure the panicked people of this country, he decided it wasn't safe to return to the White House. He basically went into hiding for the day—and he told Vice President Dick Cheney to stay put in his bunker. We were all frozen in front of our TVs, scared out of our wits, waiting for our leaders to tell us that we were going to be okay, and there was nobody home. It took Bush a couple of days to get his bearings and devise the right photo op at Ground Zero.

That was George Bush's moment of truth, and he was paralyzed. And what did he do when he'd regained his composure? He led us down the road to Iraq—a road his own father had considered disastrous when *he* was President. But Bush didn't listen to Daddy. He listened to a *higher* father. He prides himself on being faith based, not reality based. If that doesn't scare the crap out of you, I don't know what will.

A HELL OF A MESS

So here's where we stand. We're immersed in a bloody war with no plan for winning and no plan for leaving. We're running the biggest deficit in the history of the country. We're losing the manufacturing edge to Asia, while our once-great companies are getting slaughtered by health care costs. Gas prices are skyrocketing, and nobody in power has a coherent energy policy. Our schools are in trouble. Our borders are like sieves. The middle class is being squeezed every which way. These are times that cry out for leadership.

But when you look around, you've got to ask: "*Where have all the leaders gone?*" Where are the curious, creative communicators? Where are the people of character, courage, conviction, competence, and common sense? I may be a sucker for alliteration, but I think you get the point.

Name me a leader who has a better idea for homeland security than making us take off our shoes in airports and throw away our shampoo? We've spent billions of dollars building a huge new bureaucracy, and all we know how to do is react to things that have already happened.

Name me one leader who emerged from the crisis of Hurricane Katrina. Congress has yet to spend a *single* day evaluating the response to the hurricane, or demanding accountability for the decisions that were made in the crucial hours after the storm. Everyone's hunkering down, fingers crossed, hoping it doesn't happen again. Now, that's just crazy. Storms happen. Deal with it. Make a plan. Figure out what you're going to do the next time.

Name me an industry leader who is thinking creatively about how we can restore our competitive edge in manufacturing. Who would have believed that there could ever be a time when "the Big Three" referred to Japanese car companies? How did this happen—and more important, what are we going to do about it?

Name me a government leader who can articulate a plan for paying down the debt, or solving the energy crisis, or managing the health care problem. The silence is deafening. But these are the crises that are eating away at our country and milking the middle class dry.

I have news for the gang in Congress. We didn't elect you to sit on your asses and do nothing and remain silent while our democracy is being hijacked and our greatness is being replaced with mediocrity. What is everybody so afraid of? That some bobblehead on Fox News will call them a name? Give me a break. Why don't you guys show some spine for a change?

HAD ENOUGH?

Hey, I'm not trying to be the voice of gloom and doom here. I'm trying to light a fire. I'm speaking out because I have hope. I believe in America. In my lifetime I've had the privilege of living through some of America's greatest moments. I've also experienced some of our worst crises—the Great Depression, World War II, the Korean War, the Kennedy assassination, the Vietnam War, the 1970s oil crisis, and the struggles of recent years culminating with 9/11. If I've learned one thing, it's this: You don't get anywhere by standing on the sidelines waiting for somebody else to take action. Whether it's building a better car or building a better future for our children, we all have a role to play. That's the challenge I'm raising in this book. It's a call to action for people who, like me, believe in America. It's not too late, but it's getting pretty close. So let's shake off the horseshit and go to work. Let's tell 'em all *we've had enough.*

II

People and priorities: It's that simple

In my forty-eight years in the auto industry, I probably made six hundred speeches about management. Since my retirement, I've made many more. And I've always said the same thing: "Here's what management is about: Pick good people and set the right priorities." For the most part my audiences thought they were getting their money's worth. But sometimes I had to shake my head in disbelief. They're paying me for *that?*

The point is, there's nothing magic about it. People and priorities. It's that simple. This advice applies whether you're running a company or a country. If you think about it, it holds true for every organization and institution.

If we're going to figure out how to fix what's wrong with America, we should start with this tried-and-true formula. Because if the people are bad and the priorities are screwed up, nothing else works. Period.

Here's the thing I learned as a CEO. You succeed or fail based on your team. If you want to succeed, you've got to have a group of people that knows what they're doing. Vince Lombardi was a friend of mine, and he used to tell me, "Teamwork is what makes the Green Bay Packers great. People who work together will win—period. And that applies to companies and governments." But he also stressed that the raw material had to be there first. You had to start with the talent. And that brings me to our government. Don't you think we have a right to know *before* we cast our vote for President who's going to be on his team? We put all the focus on the top guy. But governing isn't just a one-man show.

I'd like you to think about this as we enter the presidential campaign season. Doesn't it strike you as a little bit strange that we don't demand that a presidential candidate introduce his team before we vote? Sure, we know the vice-presidential pick, but that's all about politics. Look at Dick Cheney. Cheney was the guy George Bush brought in to be in charge of his vice-presidential selection committee. Cheney interviewed all the candidates, studied their strengths and weaknesses, and finally presented Bush with his verdict. I can imagine him saying something like, "Well, George, I've spent months interviewing people, and I've finally come up with the very best person for the job—it's ME."

If we've learned nothing else from George Bush's presidency, we've learned that it matters who is in the cabinet. It matters who the advisors are—the people who have the President's ear. But have you noticed that when you ask a candidate to say anything whatsoever about possible appointments, you get some drivel about how it's inappropriate or premature to name names before the election. I don't get it. Why should it be such a secret?

WE SHOULD HAVE BOX SCORES

When I read the newspaper, I start with the front page, and then I go to the sports section. During the baseball season, for example, I look up the leaders in the American League and the leaders in the National League. The box scores make it easy to see who the top players are. It's all laid out: hits, runs, errors, and earned run averages.

I got to thinking, wouldn't it be great if we could do that for government? Presidential candidates could present their lineups for key posts, and we'd be able to evaluate which team had the strongest bullpen or the most home run hitters.

We could use a similar process for picking our representatives. When election time comes, we could look at our senator or congressman and say, "Well, this guy has been averaging around .220 for the last three years. Let's see if we can find a .300 hitter."

NAME THAT OFFICIAL

I've been conducting an informal survey, and I haven't met a single person who can name more than three members of the current cabinet without cheating and looking it up. This is supposed to be our national talent pool, and we don't even know who they are. I'll give you a hint. There are twenty of them, including the President's chief of staff.

But wait. What about the noncabinet members who have great influence? Shouldn't we know those names, too? Every President has a shadow cabinet, and the current occupant is no different. So let's look beyond the titles and look at who the candidate's friends are. In George Bush's administration, there is no person more influential than Karl Rove. Good old Boy Genius. When you're talking about the people who *really* have the President's ear, you have to put Rove at the top of the list, followed by Dick Cheney, Condoleezza Rice, and the woman I call "the Nanny," Karen Hughes. Until November 2006, Donald Rumsfeld was on the list, too, but he was benched after the Republicans got creamed in the election. This is the *real* power circle in the administration. It is an extremely *tight* circle, built from common ideology and personal loyalty. When the White House adopts a bunker mentality, this is the gang that's in the bunker.

You might think it's a diverse group. Two women, and one of them is black! But when it comes to diversity in action, race and gender take a backseat to ideas. In that respect, Bush's group of advisors is remarkably narrow.

CRONYISM LIVES

If the CEO of a corporation chose his department heads based on the system of paybacks we often see in government, he'd be called on the carpet. I can imagine myself at Chrysler trying to explain to the board, "Yeah, I realize that Joe has never built a car, but he helped me get a sweet mortgage rate on my home." You may chuckle, but do you realize how much of our government is run by cronies?

When the future of our country is at stake, it's not the time for paybacks. In fact, our Founding Fathers were so convinced that no President would ever stoop to such a thing that they didn't even bother to prohibit it in the Constitution. Alexander Hamilton wrote that any President "would be both ashamed and afraid" to appoint cronies — or, in his words "obsequious instruments of his pleasure." Better known as ass-kissers.

One of the most important lessons I learned in business was that if all you're getting from your team is a single point of view — usually *your* point of view — you've got to worry. You can get your own point of view for *free*.

I always kept some contrarians around — people I could count on to be devil's advocates. It kept me on my toes. For most of my career, I had a very talented car guy working for me named Harold Sperlich. Hal was an engineer and product planner, and he was also a genius. In the early 1960s, he played a big part in designing the first Ford Mustang. Hal wasn't a quiet genius, however. He was argumentative and outspoken. For him the creative process was like hand-to-hand combat. Needless to say, Henry Ford II didn't think Hal was properly deferential. He made me fire him a couple years before Henry fired *me*. Happily, Hal landed at Chrysler, and together we made things happen — first with the K-car, then with the minivan. I couldn't afford to let my ego get in the way when it came to Hal. He was usually *right*.

George Bush is notorious for appointing cronies to key positions—especially if they raised money for his campaigns, or are *friends* of people who raised money for his campaigns. He likes to make some of the appointments during recesses when he doesn't have to get congressional approval. That's a blatant misuse of presidential power.

We all know about Michael Brown ("Brownie"), whom Bush appointed to be the director of FEMA. He was an old school buddy of the former FEMA director, and Bush just accepted him at face value. Before Brownie joined FEMA, he was the commissioner of the International Arabian Horse Association—whatever the hell *that* is—and he was forced out of the job. Maybe the pressure got to him.

And God knows what compelled Bush to nominate his old Texas friend and legal advisor Harriet Meirs to the Supreme Court. He never fully explained his reasons, but he *did* say her religious faith was a factor. Yeah, she believed Bush was God.

These are examples of cronyism at high levels. You can find them just about everywhere you look. As any businessperson knows, qualifications matter. You wouldn't hire a dress designer to design your cars. You wouldn't hand over the controls of your airplane to the guy who runs the bumper cars at the amusement park. This is just basic common sense. Bush's administration is full of "Pioneers" and "Rangers"—people who raised a hundred thousand and two hundred thousand dollars respectively for his political campaigns. Sadly, in some cases, it's their *only* qualification. (Maybe *campaign finance reform* isn't such a bad idea, after all.)

I have firsthand experience of the favors game. Yeah, I

admit it. I campaigned for George Bush in 2000, even though I'd never met him. I'd known his father and mother for thirty years, and I figured he came from pretty good stock so he should be okay. (I didn't repeat the mistake in 2004.) After Bush was elected, I got a call from his chief of staff, Andy Card. He wanted to offer me an ambassadorship. Now, ambassadorships are a prime example of the payback system. Mostly it's a prestige assignment, and you get to be called Mr. (or Ms.) Ambassador for the rest of your life.

Of course, some ambassadorships are more coveted than others. I told Andy Card that I might like being the ambassador to Italy. Boy, I thought, wouldn't that be something? The son of Italian immigrants returning to his parents' homeland as an American ambassador! I have to confess I liked the idea. Unfortunately, Italy was already taken, so I passed.

Later, I was talking to Bob Dole about it. "I would have liked to be ambassador to Italy," I told him.

He laughed. "What would you want to do *that* for? Don't you already have a house in Tuscany?" That was true. I enjoy spending a few weeks there every year during grape-crushing season.

Dole explained, "If you were ambassador, your main job would be to entertain all the Texas Republican donors coming to Italy—and it would be mostly at your own expense, because those embassy budgets aren't that big. Wouldn't you rather entertain people of your own choice in Tuscany?"

I guess he had a point. But the whole experience got me wondering about what would happen if we chose ambassadors for their ability to grease the wheels of international cooperation abroad, instead of their ability to grease the wheels of political fund-raising at home.

The more people see government as an insider's game, the more cynical they get about the ability of government to achieve the common good. I read a poll recently. It said that only 5 percent of mothers wanted their kids to grow up to be President. Five percent! That's a shocking figure. Isn't it supposed to be the American dream—that *any* kid can aspire to the highest office in the land? But political life is an unpopular choice these days. I think that's because we've lost the connection between politics and public service.

Over time the distaste with Washington has eroded our talent pool. So when you're looking for competence, you're not always getting the best people. And with the cost of running campaigns, we are in real danger of electing only the wealthy and connected. In some states, you need at least $60 million to run for the Senate, or no one takes you seriously. And they're already predicting that the 2008 presidential election will have a billion-dollar price tag. You've got to ask yourself if that's what you want. And if it's not, vote for people who are committed to making a difference for the common good, not just for their *own* good.

THE NATIONAL HOT LIST

Having the right people in place will help you set the right priorities. And having the right priorities will help you choose the right people.

You can't run a company without having a business plan, so

why do you think you can run a country by the seat of your pants? For my entire career, I always kept a hot list. I updated it every week. I always believed that you should be able to write down your top priorities on a single sheet of 8½-by-11-inch paper. If you can't state a priority in fifty words or less, you're in trouble.

Do we have a national hot list? Well, that's kind of hard to say, because politicians tend to keep things pretty vague. But here's something else I'd like to see in the next campaign. After we ask, "Who's going to be on your team?" let's ask the candidates to name their top three priorities.

One, two, three. No waffling. Oh, and can we have it in *writing*, please?

Once we have the candidates' priorities, then we've got to ask, "What are the three actions you're going to take to address each of your priorities?" Let's have those in writing, too.

Look, this isn't rocket science. It's only complicated because the candidates want to *make* it complicated. We have to push for simplicity. And then, when we elect the candidate whose priorities we agree with, we have to make sure those priorities actually get addressed.

Accountability is a slippery business these days. How do you know what's actually being accomplished? Well, you have to start by looking at whether the policies and priorities are *working*. You know, *getting results*.

The job of a leader is to accomplish goals that advance the common good. Anyone can take up space. Here's the test of a leader: When he leaves office, we should be better off than when he started. It's that simple.

III

Can you show me where it's working?

Talk is cheap. Where I come from, in the auto industry, you were held brutally accountable for your programs and products. The response to any idea was, "Show me where it's working." Well, that's kind of obvious, isn't it? For example, it took us a long time to install air bags in cars because we had to figure out how to build an explosive device that didn't take your head off in the process of trying to protect you. It had to *work*. That's not happening in the political or economic realms today. Where's the accountability for results?

If you're like me, you spend a lot of time scratching your head and wondering what they're doing up there on Capitol Hill. Well, we already know that they're only working 27 percent of the time. You'd think there would be a sense of urgency when they *do* come to Washington.

Is it too much to ask our elected officials to actually solve a problem once in a while? How about even taking a stab at an

issue that matters to Americans? When pollsters ask ordinary people what they really care about, in order of importance, here's
what they say: (1) the war in Iraq, (2) jobs, (3) health care, (4)
education, and (5) energy. Those seem like reasonable priorities
to me. But in 2006, although there was plenty of posturing
about the war and the economy, when it came to legislative priorities—that is, actually *doing* something—the liveliest debates
were about side issues. In one three-month session in the United
States Senate *these* were the priorities: a constitutional amendment to ban gay marriage, a constitutional amendment to ban
flag burning, and cutting the capital gains tax. Our senators had
time to debate flag burning for three days, but no time to tackle
health care, energy, jobs, or anything else Americans care about.
Since 1777, there have been only forty-five documented cases of
flag burning. But since 2000, nearly three million manufacturing jobs have gone up in smoke, and it wasn't because people
were burning flags. No wonder only 25 percent of Americans
approve of the job Congress is doing.

It's too soon to say whether or not things will improve
under Democratic leadership. But neither side has shown a
commitment to breaking gridlock in recent years, so I'm not very
optimistic.

The Constitution of the United States was drafted in fewer
than one hundred working days. That was quite an accom-
plishment. It's fair to ask our legislators, "What have you done
for us lately? What can you show us that's working?"

CAN YOU SHOW ME WHERE IT'S WORKING?

Nobody even asks the question, so I guess I will.

- Homeland security. Where is it working?
- The permanent tax cut. Where is it working?
- No Child Left Behind. Where is it working?
- The Patriot Act. Where is it working?
- Welfare reform. Where is it working?

That's just the short list. And whatever happened to Social Security reform? Immigration reform? Health care reform? Why is it so hard to find out what's actually getting *done?* Could it be because nothing *is* getting done? I hope not, but I'm not too sure.

WHEN IN DOUBT, BUILD A BUREAUCRACY

There's one thing the folks on Capitol Hill *do* seem to be good at: building bureaucracies. I have to tell you, I really threw up my hands in despair the day they announced the creation of the Department of Homeland Security. At the very moment when we most needed to be lean and mean, we decided to undertake the largest government reorganization in *fifty years!* The DHS consolidated twenty-two agencies and nearly two hundred thousand federal employees under its vast umbrella.

What kind of job is the Department of Homeland Security

doing? How is it spending its fifty-billion-dollar-a-year budget? Are we safer now than we were before 9/11? *Yes or no?* The bipartisan 9/11 Commission has given the Department of Homeland Security a *failing* grade (five Fs, twelve Ds, and two incompletes) for not making headway on the commission's key recommendations for keeping us safer. Specifically, the commission cites:

- No headway on federal agencies sharing intelligence and terrorism information.
- No improvement in airline-passenger prescreening.
- No improvement on nuclear power plant security. (In mock terrorist incidents, over half the plants failed.)
- Little improvement in border security.

If I'd brought home a report card like that, my father would have taken me to the woodshed. He insisted on straight As and accepted no excuses. He taught me that striving for excellence was my ticket to the American dream. Maybe that ideal has been lost.

For most of us, the only experience we have with the Department of Homeland Security is when we go to an airport. After 9/11, air safety was job one. Right? Well, they took away our nail clippers and our liquids. They reinforced cockpit doors—which was actually a smart thing to do. And they put air marshals on planes. We all feel safer knowing there might be an air marshal on our plane.

But wait a minute. According to a group of air marshals who publicly complained about the program, it's so transparent that even little kids can identify them. Maybe it's the *dress code*.

Or maybe it's the fact that air marshals have to publicly check in and show their credentials *twice* before they get on the plane. First at the metal detectors, and then at the gate. And once they get on board, they have to visit the cockpit and show their credentials to the pilot. They do everything but personally introduce themselves to the passengers. By the time an air marshal takes his seat, the only people on board who haven't pegged him are either zoned out on their iPods or asleep.

The biggest problem with airport security is that it's *reactive*, not *proactive*. Threat of shoe bombs? Everyone takes off their shoes. Threat of liquid explosives? Everyone dumps their mouthwash and deodorant. I hope nobody tries to get past security with explosives hidden in a book, or you won't be reading this on your flight to Cincinnati.

PLENTY OF RHETORIC, LITTLE ACTION

I'm starting to get the suspicion that maybe the point of government is the *bureaucracy*, not the results. I started thinking about all the great crusades we've had in the last forty years. Politicians like to wage these so-called wars with great fanfare. We've declared war on poverty, war on drugs, war on big government, war on crime—just to name a few. That's in addition to our *real* wars. But have you ever noticed that once the big campaign is rolled out and the politicians have all patted each other on the back, we never hear about it again? Did we win? Did we lose? Does anybody know?

The war on drugs was launched *thirty-six* years ago. If

they're not careful, it's going to turn into the hundred-year war. How're we doing? We spend around $40 billion a year fighting the war on drugs. A conservative estimate of the total amount we've spent would be around *one trillion dollars*. So, are we winning? Well, we lock up about two million people a year—mostly drug users. But every expert analysis of our progress shows the same thing: After thirty-six years, we have not reduced the *quantity* of drugs or the *consumption* of drugs one lousy percentage point.

Wake up, fellas. We've lost the war on drugs. But let any politician even *suggest* that we try a different strategy and he gets accused of being *soft* on drugs. It's a hell of a way to run a war.

A RADICAL PROPOSAL

In Congress they pass law after law. They never really stop to look at the effects of the laws they pass. They just pass another one. They keep grinding out that sausage, and no one goes back and says, "Last year we budgeted $2 billion for that program. Did it work? Did we get a bang for our buck?" There's no time for oversight. They're already moving on to the next $2 billion. Is anyone surprised that 80 percent of Americans say our government is *broken*?

So I have a proposal, and I know it's a little radical, but hear me out. I'd like to give Congress a year off. That's right. One year. I'd send them to a quiet place where they wouldn't be distracted—maybe a nice convention center on Lake Michigan. And I'd tell them, "For the next year your job is NOT to pass any new laws or spend any new money. Your job is to evaluate what you've already done. Take each one of the hundreds of bills you've passed in the last three years, and show where it's working. And if it's *not* working, pull the plug on it.

"Don't worry about being away from Washington for a year. Most people won't even know you're gone. We'll have someone answer the phones and take messages. We'll call you if anything really urgent comes up." But come to think of it, what could be more urgent than figuring out how to run a country that works?

IV

Aren't we supposed to be the *good* guys?

I've had a new word added to my vocabulary. The word is *waterboarding*. I kind of wish I'd never heard of it. No, it's not a new sport. It's a method of torture that involves dunking a prisoner underwater until he almost drowns, then pulling him up for air—and repeating the process until he talks. It can give you nightmares if you spend too much time thinking about methods of torture. But what *really* gives me nightmares is finding out that the United States is the one doing the torturing.

Hey, aren't we supposed to be the *good* guys?

Look, I'm not naïve. I know war is hell. As General George Patton used to remind his troops during World War II, war is about *killing*. It's bloody. But even in war, our nation has always chosen to uphold a certain moral code. We have declared that we are not going to *become* the evil we are fighting. I'd like someone to explain to me how torturing prisoners has become the American way.

And don't try to sell me that line of bull about how September 11 changed the rules of the game. September 11 was a horrible day. It was an act of unimaginable evil. But I just don't buy it that because a group of terrorists attacked us on September 11, we're suddenly justified in torturing people. I don't buy it that it's patriotic to pull people off the street and hold them indefinitely—and maybe *forever*—without even having to tell them why. Or ship them off to secret prisons in Eastern Europe. That might be worse than torture.

It's pretty sad to think we've come to this point. It makes you nostalgic for the leaders of the past.

I can still remember how things were right after we defeated the Nazis in World War II. We had captured some of Hitler's top henchmen, and everyone was wondering what we were going to do with them. These were guys who had ordered the murder of millions of innocent people in concentration camps. These were guys who had conducted cruel medical experiments on little children. They were evil, in the truest sense of the word. A lot of people thought we should just line them up and shoot them, or turn them over to the concentration camp survivors and let them be torn apart. Emotions ran pretty high. Would anyone really have objected to torturing those sons of bitches? I doubt it. But we had leaders then who reminded us of our higher ideals. Winston Churchill and Harry Truman insisted on holding the Nuremberg Trials. Think about it. We took the worst criminals of our times and we put them in a court of law. We gave them lawyers. We didn't *become* the evil we were fighting.

I also remember a few years later when the United States signed on to the Geneva Conventions. Who were the most enthusiastic supporters of the Geneva Conventions? Well, it might surprise you to know that they were two great military heroes—General Douglas MacArthur and Dwight D. Eisenhower. You wouldn't call them pansies or bleeding hearts. They were speaking from experience. They'd seen how American soldiers were tortured and murdered in Japanese prison camps. The Geneva Conventions were meant to protect our soldiers in captivity. From that day forward, even during the Vietnam War when the North Vietnamese refused to abide by the Geneva Conventions, *we* always did.

Until now.

Vice President Cheney has argued in favor of torture. He said, "We have to work through, *sort of*, the dark side."

Sort of the dark side? Hey, I have news for Cheney. There's no *sort of* about it. Torture *is* the dark side.

I can't believe we're even having a discussion about whether it's okay to torture prisoners. The people who think torture is okay seem to get most of their examples from the movies or TV dramas. They always give some outlandish example, like, if you were holding a guy who knew of a plot to blow up America, wouldn't torture be justified to get information? The problem is, that's not what is really happening. What's really happening is that you've got a bunch of guys who were rounded up in Afghanistan, handed over to the U.S. military by locals, and shipped off to Guantánamo. To my knowledge, there's not one leader of Al Qaeda in the bunch. Am I the only one who's embarrassed that they call Guantánamo the American *gulag*?

By the way, morality aside, I think we have to ask this question—*even* when we're talking about torture: *Does it work?*

Most experts on the subject say that under torture a prisoner will tell you anything you want to hear. But it won't necessarily be true. And that's what's really pathetic about this whole mess. We're trashing our principles, and we're not even getting anything in return.

I WANT MY COUNTRY BACK

When I say I'm proud to be an American, what I mean is that I'm proud to live in a nation that is a force for good in the world. I'm proud to live in a nation that values human life. I'm proud to live in a nation where we "hold these truths to be self-evident: that all men are created equal, that they are endowed by their Creator with certain unalienable rights, that among these are Life, Liberty and the pursuit of Happiness."

We don't say "*some*" men. We don't say "except when we decide you're evil." How did we lose our way?

LET'S START BY TONING DOWN THE RHETORIC

Words matter. Winston Churchill, one of the great orators of the twentieth century, put it this way: "Of all the talents bestowed upon men, none is so precious as the gift of oratory. Abandoned by his party, betrayed by his friends, stripped of his office, whoever can command this power is still formidable."

Words can inspire. They can lift us to heights we never

dreamed possible. Words can also provoke fear and rage. They can pound people into the ground.

A true leader always strives to inspire. That doesn't mean he can't express outrage. But he motivates people to act by appealing to the *good* in their hearts, not the *evil* in the hearts of others. He motivates people with possibility, not with threats. President Dwight Eisenhower once said, "You don't lead by hitting people over the head. That's assault, not leadership."

If you want to know how we got to the point of condoning torture, all you have to do is look at the trail of rhetoric from our leader:

> *Axis of evil*
> *Mushroom cloud*
> *Shock and awe*
> *Wanted, dead or alive*
> *Ticking time bombs*
> *Enemies of freedom*
> *The forces of darkness and tyranny*
> *You're with us or against us*
> *Bring 'em on*

Do you start to see a theme here? We can't bully the world into submission. We can't expect to win cooperation by calling people evil. You don't have to *talk* tough in order to *be* tough. I have a simple piece of advice for President Bush: Fire the goddamned speechwriters!

Look, this planet is a crowded place, and the only way we're going to survive is to learn to get along with one another.

Now, you can decide that the way to lead is to knock off all the people you think are against you, but that's never really worked, has it? And it's not what democracy is all about.

It's time to get back to basics. What *is* democracy, anyway? Who *are* we as a people? Are we willing to do what it takes to be the good guys?

V

How much do we love democracy?

My parents, Nicola and Antoinette Iacocca, belonged to that amazing wave of Italian immigration that helped transform America into the land of prosperity. As immigrants, my parents had a reverence for this country that you seldom see today. When my sister Delma and I were kids, Mom and Pop took us to visit the Statue of Liberty twice. We piled into Pop's beat-up old Ford and drove from Allentown, Pennsylvania, to New York City—which took a long time in those days. I remember walking with my father up the 354 stairs to the crown, huffing and puffing a little, but excited about the adventure. Standing in the crown of the Statue of Liberty, Pop pointed down at the harbor and told me about the thrill of seeing America for the first time.

I'm ashamed to admit that when I became a father, I didn't think to take my girls to see Lady Liberty. When we visited New York City, we were too busy going to Broadway shows, eating at great restaurants, and touring museums.

It's a sad thing that complacency can set in so fast. As I look around me today, I see that our democracy has become a little worn, a little shabby. The rhetoric is still there, but the passion has wilted. Do we still love democracy? Do we have any idea what democracy really means?

How about a regime change right here in the United States? Instead of trying to establish democracy in countries that don't want it, why not try to *reestablish* democracy where we've lost it?

Are you wondering, "Lee, what are you talking about? I have my SUPPORT THE TROOPS bumper sticker and my yellow-ribbon window decal. I have an American flag waving proudly from my car antenna. I *love* this country."

And I'll come right back at you with a very simple question: Did you vote in last fall's election?

Democracy thrives on two factors: free elections and open discourse. How are we doing? Not so hot.

VOTING—A RIGHT OR A DUTY?

It drives me crazy that Americans don't vote. We should be ashamed. It is plain hypocrisy for us to hold up our system of government as the best there is, yet fail to practice the most fundamental action of a free people—*voting*.

It's embarrassing that the United States has one of the worst voting records in the free world. In the last presidential election, about 45 percent of those eligible cast a vote. Compare that to recent free elections in other countries:

Australia:	96%
Indonesia:	93%
Belgium:	91%
South Africa:	89%
Ukraine:	86%
Canada:	73%

Are you embarrassed yet?

I have to wonder how much difference it would make if voting was mandatory—like paying taxes. Now, before you get your hackles up and start hollering that mandatory elections would not be free, hear me out.

In some countries, voting is considered not just a *right*, but a *duty* of living in a democracy. The argument is that a government is more representative when a larger percentage of the population votes. About thirty countries have some form of mandatory voting, with various (usually mild) penalties for the slackers. In Belgium, if you don't vote in at least four elections within a fifteen-year period, you get kicked off the voter rolls. In Greece, you may have a hard time getting a driver's license or a passport if you don't vote. In Singapore, you're removed from the voter register and must reapply and give a good reason for not having voted. And in several countries, small fines are imposed.

These penalties are not exactly draconian, but they have one advantage: They remind people that freedom is not *free*.

What if the United States passed a law that you had to vote in order to be eligible for certain tax cuts? That would make people sit up and take notice! Instead of debating flag burning, maybe Congress could spend a day or two talking about *that*. At least it would have some relevance to the practice of democracy.

Unfortunately, we bend over backward in the opposite direction—making it *harder*, not easier, for people to vote.

Across the nation, there are many impediments to voting, including voter ID statutes, broken voting machines, and long lines at the polls. Low voter turnout means more empty rhetoric during election season. Everyone tries to appeal to the "base"—those people who are ideologically passionate about one side or the other, and will show up to vote no matter what.

I'll bet that the people who would object the most vehemently to any form of mandatory voting would be our elected officials. The sad fact is that most of them don't *want* more people to vote. They might have to show results for a change. They prefer the cozy, inbred system where 98 percent of all incumbents are reelected. It's called a *stacked deck*.

When I'm at a dinner party and someone says, "I didn't vote in the last election, but here's what I think," I tune them out quick. What if we all did that? Even if we didn't make voting mandatory in the United States, maybe we could try to exert some *social* pressure. For example:

- What if your child wouldn't be eligible for that fancy preschool if you didn't vote?
- What if your boss would be less inclined to give you a raise if you didn't vote?
- What if people didn't shop at your store if you didn't vote?

- What if you couldn't appear on *American Idol* if you didn't vote?
- What if people snubbed you at barbecues or dinner parties if you didn't vote?

Social pressure is a great motivator. We should try it.

DARE TO SPEAK OUT

Besides voting, the other cornerstone of democracy is open discourse and debate. But most politicians are downright squeamish about speaking out and rocking the boat. I hate to think of where we'd be if our Founding Fathers hadn't slugged it out over what kind of a constitution we were going to have.

You might argue that the Democrats won the 2006 election because they spoke out against the war. But the Democrats only started speaking out when the polls showed them it was absolutely safe to do so. Where were they in 2005 or in 2004? Where were they before we got into this war? As I recall, there was only one man who took it on the chin and spoke out against the war before it was politically expedient. That man is John Murtha.

Let me tell you about John Murtha. He's the Democratic congressman from Johnstown, Pennsylvania, and he also happens to be a good friend of mine. In 1966, John volunteered for service in Vietnam. As a captain in the Marine Corps he received the Bronze Star, two Purple Hearts, and the Navy Distinguished Service Medal. He ran for Congress in 1974 and has served there ever since. He's what you'd call a true patriot.

He's also been a true friend to soldiers, and one of the most credible guys in Congress on matters of war. Every administration, Republican and Democrat, has listened to him on military matters. Until this administration.

Murtha voted to go to war in Iraq, but as the years passed he got pretty riled up about the disastrous course of the war, and he decided he couldn't stay silent for another minute. Kids were dying and he decided he had to speak up and demand that we bring the troops home. He was one of the few to do so before it was politically "safe."

How did the Bush administration respond? Karl Rove tried to "Swift-boat" Murtha. *Swift-boating* is the new term used to describe a dirty campaign that tries to paint a war hero as unpatriotic. It originated with another war hero, John Kerry. Running for President against the AWOL National Guardsman in Chief, George Bush, Kerry watched his Swift-boat heroism during the Vietnam War turned into something shameful and cowardly. It was probably the ugliest thing I've ever seen in politics—and that's saying a lot. I was disgusted by it, and I tried to convince Kerry to fight back. "These guys are playing dirty," I told him. "It's time for you to aim a few blows below the belt, if that's what it takes, or they're going to run right over you." He refused, and I think that's why he lost the election. People started saying, "If he can't stick up for *himself*, how can we expect him to stick up for *us*."

These guys have put everyone on notice: "Criticize the war and we'll ruin you." They did it with Max Cleland, another war hero. Max is in a wheelchair. Do they think he's *faking* it? They did it with Kerry. And they came after Murtha. Karl Rove could smear Mother Teresa—he's that devious. When will we stand up and say, "Enough!"

I take it personally when our government tries to ruin a man who speaks his mind.

ABSOLUTE POWER CORRUPTS

We pride ourselves on our two-party system. But the way it stands now, each of the two main political parties tries to gain *all* the power. They each want to create a one-party system, because it's so much easier to rule when everyone's on the same side. The Republicans mostly succeeded in having a one-party system during the first six years of Bush's administration. They turned Congress into a big dissent-free zone. If you don't believe me, just look at Bush's record of vetoes. When Congress passes a law that the President disagrees with, he can veto it. Then if Congress can scrape together enough votes (two-thirds), it can override the veto. This process is called the separation of powers.

If the process is working, you expect to see a lot of vetoes in the course of a President's term, although some Presidents have gotten carried away. They used to call Truman "Harry S. Veto." He vetoed 250 bills during his presidency—but he didn't even come *close* to FDR's record of 635. Recent presidents have calmed down somewhat. Reagan vetoed 78 bills, Bush senior 44, and Clinton 37.

And the current President? *One* veto. Wait, you say, am I hearing right? Just *one*? That's right. In six-plus years, George Bush disagreed with Congress exactly once. In case you don't get the significance of that, let me spell it out: Under Bush, the executive and legislative branches of our government merged into one. Bush didn't veto legislation because it was basically *his* legislation to begin with.

BRING BACK THE CONSTITUTION

We don't have to fly by the seat of our pants. We have a blueprint. It's called the United States Constitution. But we've got to stay vigilant, because when people get into power in Washington, they tend to work hard to get around constitutional provisions.

Bush did that with wiretapping. His attorney general, Alberto Gonzales, assured him that a "war President" didn't have to abide by the Fourth Amendment, which guarantees the citizens of the United States the right to privacy. They spied on us, and when people complained they said, "What do you have to hide?" That's one of the oldest tricks in the book. Finally, a federal judge in Detroit named Anna Diggs Taylor called a halt to the illegal wiretapping, taking a jab at the imperial Bush presidency, declaring, "There are no hereditary kings in America." I wonder if Bush was surprised to hear that.

When you stop and think about it, the Constitution is like the Bible. You don't really have to read it every day to know what's in it. You don't have to memorize every word to know what it stands for.

The Constitution is a tool, and a blueprint, and a process that we have to use every day to preserve our great democracy. Its words were hammered out by pragmatists—a group of men who understood that democracy doesn't happen because of starry-eyed idealism, but through a process of tedious negotiation and compromise.

And for 230 years it has worked. The real genius of the Constitution, it seems to me, is that it has retained its fundamental values while giving us the freedom to adapt to the times. You can read the Constitution all day long and you won't find an answer to most of the big problems and questions we face today. There's nothing in it to tell us how to handle terrorism, or the energy crisis, or health care, or stem cell research, or the drug war. But through the Constitution, we intrinsically understand who we are. We say, "This is what we stand for." Its meaning should be imprinted on every heart. It should come to mind every time we vote.

PAUSE TO LISTEN . . . AND THINK

During the coming year, you will be asked to form an opinion about who should be our next President. In the process, you'll be bombarded by media coverage on a minute-to-minute basis. All that coverage will not necessarily produce much valuable information. The media likes the horse-race aspect of campaigns—who's up, who's down, who flubs, who cries. But I hope with the world aflame, you'll bypass the silly season and take your obligation seriously.

We have so much media these days, and it moves so fast, it's easy to get left with impressions that aren't accurate. You can miss the facts if you're rapid-clicking your remote. I found this out the hard way a few years back when my name appeared in two stories that had nothing to do with me. I call it being screwed by juxtaposition.

The first story involved Heidi Fleiss, the infamous Hollywood madam. I was passing by the TV one day, and it was turned on to an interview with Heidi. She was describing the thousand-dollar fee that she'd charged for an evening with one of her girls.

The interviewer asked, "If a guy pays a thousand dollars for an evening, does he pick up the dinner tab, too?"

Heidi said, "Well, that depends. Let's say, for example, it was Lee Iacocca . . ."

What? I never heard the rest of the sentence because my phone started ringing off the hook. For weeks after, people would sidle up to me and whisper, "Hey, I hear you're in Heidi's black book." My denials fell on deaf ears. Heidi Fleiss had said my name, and that was good enough for them.

Then, a couple months later, it happened again. This was during the time when the FBI was trying to catch the Unabomber. You might remember that they had a sketch of a suspect wearing a hooded sweatshirt, large sunglasses, and a mustache. One day, I was watching the news and an FBI specialist was demonstrating to a reporter how easy it is to change one's identity. He took the Unabomber sketch and removed the hooded sweatshirt. Then he erased the mustache. And finally he took off the sunglasses.

"Hey," the TV reporter exclaimed, "that's Lee Iacocca!"

Once again, my phone started ringing off the hook. "Lee, someone said you were involved with the Unabomber . . ."

I was glad about one thing—I wasn't running for political office. I assure you, had I been a candidate, I would have spent 90 percent of my time either explaining what I was doing in Heidi Fleiss's black book, or trying to prove I wasn't the Unabomber.

So I caution you to avoid jumping to conclusions or basing your vote on quick impressions. Chances are, they'll be wrong.

HOW TO PICK A LEADER

The goal is to vote for a leader. How can you tell if a candidate is the kind of leader we need? Here's a good place to start. Give him or her my Nine Cs test. That'll tell you right away if the person should even be in the running.

I've already started applying the Nine Cs to the current crop of potential candidates, and as I look at some of the early front-runners, I've started to form an opinion. Mind you, this is *my* opinion. You may see it differently. But the point is, you have to read, listen, and educate yourself. Think it through on your own. Do some digging.

I'm not going to try to handicap the election. I've never been that good at the track. But I thought you might find it helpful to see how I've applied the Nine Cs to some of these folks.

John McCain has shown COURAGE and CHARACTER in the worst CRISIS imaginable—being a prisoner of war. I think we've been so disappointed in our leaders that we have a hunger for people we can look up to for their strength and heroism, and that is why McCain holds a special place in many people's hearts. But politically he has changed his position so many times, you have to ask if he really has political CONVICTION. He has a habit of being both for and against an issue, depending on the audience (example: abortion). While he shows a willingness to compromise, which is a good thing, his compromises can feel like caving in (examples: campaign finance reform and the torture act). The media needs to push McCain on his contradictory stands and help us get a real idea of what he would do in office.

In the Senate, McCain has demonstrated that he can work across party lines, and we could really use a President who can unite the parties. However, I was a little disturbed to learn that he's hired Terry Nelson to be his campaign manager. Nelson is known for below-the-belt politics. He was responsible for the famous "bimbo" ad that defeated Harold Ford, Jr., in the 2006 Tennessee Senate race. What does it say about John McCain that he's willing to make that kind of person the head of his team? I think we should ask him.

Rudy Giuliani earned the title "America's mayor" for showing remarkable cool and COURAGE under pressure during the CRISIS of 9/11. You can't take that away from him. But as I've watched the clamor building for his candidacy, I've noticed that people seem to be in love with the image, and aren't so interested in looking at Rudy's record before 9/11. Who is Rudy Giuliani? He wasn't born on 9/11. I've known Rudy personally for many years, and he can be rigid and punitive in his governing style. Many New Yorkers feel he was a divisive mayor. In fact, Rudy's popularity rating on September 11 was pretty low. While mayor of New York City, Rudy had a "my way or the highway" attitude that kind of reminds me of George W. Bush—

which is alarming. And he isn't known for his COMMUNICA-TION skills. (Perhaps the best example of poor communication skills is that he announced at a press conference he was leaving his wife—*before* he told her.) And what about COMPE-TENCE? It was Rudy Giuliani who insisted, against all advice, to locate New York City's crisis coordination center at the World Trade Center, in spite of the 1993 bombing. That decision may have contributed to the chaos on 9/11.

What kind of team would Rudy put together? His associations raise some issues about his CHARACTER. Some of them have corruption problems. Former police commissioner Bernie Kerik is the most famous. I hope the media asks Rudy to account for some of his actions and associations while mayor—*before* 9/11.

Mitt Romney: I think of Romney as a local boy—and he *was* just a boy when I knew his parents, George and Lenore. They were very close neighbors of ours in Bloomfield Hills, Michigan. George Romney, as you may recall, was president of American Motors and served as governor of Michigan during some critical periods. I always admired the guy. He was a smart businessman (he coined the term "gas guzzler"), and like most Mormons I've known, he believed in giving something back to the community through public service. So, what do I think of George's son? Like his father, Mitt Romney spent two years as a missionary before he started his career. That says something about his CHARACTER. He's proved himself to be a talented businessman, and while he didn't set the world on fire as a one-term governor of Massachusetts, he was COMPETENT. I'd say Romney's biggest challenge is to have the COURAGE of his

CONVICTIONS. He's always been a political moderate, but that doesn't play too well with the Republican base.

Hillary Clinton is a smart woman, and even her detractors acknowledge that she has shown COMMON SENSE and COMPETENCE in the Senate. I have no doubt that we're ready to have a woman President. But is Hillary the one? There is always a question mark about CHARACTER and CONVICTION hanging over her head. She's a bit too slick and politically expedient, and her movement to the center leaves her without a strong political identity. Her style of COMMUNICATION is always very careful, as if she's weighing the pros and cons of each word she utters. People often ask, "What does Hillary believe in?" I don't think that question has been answered.

Hillary has a huge team of advisors, with a core of loyalists that have been with her for ten to fifteen years. Her number one teammate is Bill Clinton, and maybe that's Hillary's biggest problem. Is America ready for the weird scenario of having the Clintons back in the White House in a reversal of roles? I try to be open-minded, but that's a lot to get your head around. Would a Hillary Clinton presidency distract from the focus on the important issues we have to face? The media needs to press Hillary on why she wants to be President, and why she thinks she's the best person for the job.

Joe Biden is a career public servant. I've known Joe for many years, and I like the guy. He has many of the qualities that make a leader. He is COMPETENT, CREATIVE, and CURIOUS. He has COMMON SENSE. Not much CHARISMA, though. A lot of people think Biden is too plodding, but in my opinion this is a bum rap. And maybe what we really need this time around is someone who knows what he or she is doing. I've seen Joe inspire small groups of people with his simple command of facts and his logic. He's not afraid to tell people what he thinks. There's some great experience in that man—much of it in foreign affairs—if we're willing to take advantage of it.

Joe's biggest challenge is that despite a long career in the Senate, he's not that well known across the country. If he wants to convince us he's ready to lead the nation, he'll have to get outside his cozy insider's world and COMMUNICATE his plan in a way that makes people pay attention.

Barack Obama is one of those stars who seem to come from nowhere to capture the imagination of the nation. What's not to like about this guy? He has CHARISMA and CONVICTION, and obviously he has strong COMMUNICATION skills. In my opinion, his race isn't an issue. We're as ready to elect a black man as we are to elect a woman. But is Obama the one? Is he COMPETENT to be President? He lacks experience in national government, and the media needs to push him on how he would lead—especially in foreign affairs. However, lack of experience isn't always an insurmountable barrier. Look at the mess George Bush's experienced team of Cheney and Rumsfeld made of things. But Obama is going to have to get very specific about what he would do and who would be on his team, in order for us to have enough confidence in him.

John Edwards is a very appealing guy, and I think he's shown CHARACTER in his choice of issues. Let's face it: Standing up for the poor isn't the best way to raise money for your candidacy. Right now, Edwards is the only real populist in the race. He can COMMUNICATE, and has some star power, which can also make him look a bit slick. He's had plenty of CRISIS in his life—the death of a child, and a wife with breast cancer—and his response has been inspirational. But is he COMPETENT to be President? Edwards was only in the Senate for one term before dropping out to run with Kerry.

One of the best things about John Edwards is his wife Elizabeth. She's his closest advisor, and pretty much everyone agrees that she's fantastic. His campaign manager is former congressman David Bonior from Michigan, who is a strong labor loyalist. I guess this shows where Edwards stands on domestic policy. Now let's ask questions about his foreign policy plan.

Bill Richardson: I met Bill Richardson a couple of times when we were promoting NAFTA. He's very smart, and he has a keen understanding of foreign relations—which is extremely important for a presidential candidate today. I'd say Richardson's greatest strength is that he's a strong COMMUNICATOR. He has the mind and heart of a negotiator, and I'm struck by how respectful he is of other nations—friends and foes alike. He also has an easygoing COMMON SENSE that is comforting in an age when ideologues rule the roost. And don't forget, Richardson is extremely experienced, with proven COMPETENCE. He has worn many hats in government: He served in Congress, he was a cabinet member and an ambassador under Clinton, and he's now governor of New Mexico. His biggest challenge will be getting his message out in a crowded field.

Others will come and go in the next year. Some of these frontrunners will fade, and some will grow stronger. But here's the key: Whatever the lineup, it is our obligation to look beyond appearances and sound bites, and do the hard work of choosing a leader. We can't afford to get it wrong this time.

Here's another caution. Recently, I saw a poll showing that 30 percent of Americans think "the time is right" for a business leader in the White House. Every couple of election cycles, people decide they're tired of politicians and they look to the business world. That's not necessarily such a bad thing. But you've got to realize that a business is not a democracy, so business leaders can get pretty frustrated with the immense bureaucracy and its glacial pace. And if you're a CEO, you don't have to worry too much about being politically correct.

Back in 1987, a lot of people were urging me to run for president in 1988. Committees were formed, money was raised, bumper stickers were produced (I LIKE I). I took it seriously. I went to visit my friend Tip O'Neill in Cape Cod to ask for his advice.

"Tip," I said, "they want me to run for president."

He laughed. "President of *what*?"

Tip set me straight. He said, "You're used to running a big corporation. When you make a decision in the morning, you either earn a profit that day or you don't. You can't run a government that way. It would drive you crazy. You wouldn't last a year. You'd have a heart attack because of the frustration. And if you did manage to live through the first year, you'd probably be assassinated in the second year because you'd push the envelope too far."

I said, "Thanks for the *tip*, Tip." I gave back the money and bowed out.

The point is, you can be a success in business and not have

the temperament to be president. For myself, I concluded long ago that to run for President you've got to be overambitious or just plain crazy.

American democracy is a wonderful thing. Because no matter what they tell you, the American people, vote by vote, can create whatever we want to create. It's all in our hands. But we have to stay alert and keep ourselves informed. Democracy isn't a spectator sport.

Mark your calendar for November 11, 2008, and plan to vote. Casting your vote is an act of leadership, because you're making a choice that will decide the future of this country. Step up to the booth. Take on the challenge. Anyone can be a leader, including you.

PART TWO

WHERE HAVE ALL OUR FRIENDS GONE?

VI

Will the *real* leader of the free world please stand up?

My father had a talent for making friends. When I was a kid, our house was always bustling. Every Sunday after church, it was crowded with family and friends, laughing, eating pasta, and drinking red wine. My father lit up those gatherings. Even during tough times, it was hard to feel gloomy when you were around him. I think what drew people to my father was his optimism. He loved life, and he hated to see anyone down in the dumps. If you were feeling low, he'd say, "Just wait. The sun's gonna come out. It always does." He meant it, too. And he was *right*.

Pop used to tell me, "If when you die you've got five real friends, you've had a great life." He wanted me to see that *people* were more important than anything else. In fact, I think what he loved most about America was the way it opened its arms to the world.

If Pop were alive today, he'd be pretty upset to see how few friends America seems to have right now. I have to admit it gets kind of depressing for me, too. Everyone wants to be liked, and it feels lousy when you're not. You get used to having people admire your country and want to emulate you. I always took it for granted that the U.S.A. was out in front leading the pack, and that our President was the leader of the free world. It wasn't that other countries necessarily wanted to have democracies just like ours, or to take their marching orders from our President. It was more a recognition that the United States was a good friend to have, especially in times of crisis. Anyone who lived through World War II knows what I'm talking about. We were the free world's best friend. And then, after the war, we did something *really* amazing: We turned our enemies into friends, too, by helping them rebuild their countries.

I've got to wonder if anyone out there still thinks our President is the leader of the free world. And what is the free world? Well, it might surprise you to know that the term *free world* is a little bit outdated. It was a designation created during the cold war era. Believe me, those were simpler times! There was the *Communist* world and there was the *free* world. Today, there could be many definitions of the free world, having nothing to do with democracy. We form alliances with other nations for a variety of reasons. We're trading partners, lenders, and borrowers. We come together to address common concerns such as poverty, disease, and global warming. We help each other through natural disasters. Sometimes we form wartime coalitions. But the old idea that there's a big line separating the open, free societies from the closed, repressive societies just doesn't play too well anymore.

It would be much easier if there *were* such a thing as an axis of evil and an axis of good. But the lines are awfully blurred. It gets a little confusing when one year you see the United States supporting a regime like Saddam Hussein's (as we did during the Iran-Iraq war) and the next year we're calling him an evil dictator. Sometimes we have trouble figuring out who our friends are, who we're supposed to be leading, and where we're supposed to be leading them *to*.

ALLIES VERSUS ENEMIES

When you're a kid there's always a hierarchy in every group. And usually there's one kid in particular who's the big cheese. He always has to have things his way, and the others tend to defer to him. They want to please him, because if they don't, he threatens to take his marbles and go home — or *worse*. America is getting a little bit like that. We're nice enough if you play by our rules, but you never want to cross us.

Look what happened to France. France has been America's friend since the beginning. If it weren't for France's help, we probably wouldn't have made it as a country in the first place. We've repaid the favor over time, most notably by coming to France's aid during World War I and World War II. So when France declared that it wasn't so *willing* to join Bush's "Coalition of the Willing," a lot of Americans saw it as an act of betrayal. I can't tell you how many times I heard people say something along the lines of, "We saved them in World War II, and *this* is the thanks we get." Well, it would take a lot more words than I want to expend trying to explain why that attitude was pure baloney, but who cares about common sense when you've got righteous indignation on your side? Suddenly our country was consumed with an anti-French fervor. It reached its peak of absurdity the day Congress announced that the French fries in its three House cafeterias would henceforth be known as *"Freedom* fries." (Take a good look, folks. This is an example of your tax dollars at work.)

Wisely, France did not offer an official response, except to mention that French fries actually come from *Belgium.* And luckily, we didn't go all out in banning the word *French* from our vocabulary, or you would have been "freedom-kissing" your girlfriend and eating "freedom toast" for breakfast.

Freedom fries lasted about three years, until the House cafeterias *quietly* restored the original *French fries* to the menu. But even to this day, there are a lot of hard feelings toward the French. This doesn't make any sense to me. There's little doubt in my mind that if the United States had a legitimate need, France would be on our side—just like it was when the President's father made the call for a Persian Gulf war coalition in 1991. France responded by sending thousands of troops.

One thing you learn if you live long enough is how to tell the difference between a *true* friend and a fair-weather friend. Most of us learn the hard way. I'll never forget when I got fired from Ford. There was a guy who'd been one of my best friends in the company for twenty-five years. We played poker together every Friday night. Our families were close. We even took vacations together. But after I was fired, he never even called. Boy, *that* was a bitter pill to swallow.

A leader has to know who his *true* friends are, and it's not always the ones who agree with everything or follow you blindly. With a true friend, there's got to be equality. You share the good times and you share the bad times. There's got to be respect. If your friend takes a principled position for the other side, you don't have to like it, but you don't call him names, either. These basic rules apply on the world stage as much as they do in your personal life.

I wish we could lower our voices and get rid of the tootin', shootin' cowboy mentality. It's not a weakness to admit the other guy has a point once in a while.

LEADERSHIP ON THE WORLD STAGE

What does it mean to be a world leader today? And especially, what does global leadership mean for the American President? When I started thinking about it, I realized that I'd lived through the administrations of twelve Presidents, and I've actually *met* nine of them. I'd say that four of them really excelled at being world leaders. The first two, Roosevelt and Truman, are obvious.

It is almost impossible to imagine a President today who could exert the kind of leadership Roosevelt demonstrated in getting major programs through Congress, such as Social Security, the Securities and Exchange Commission, the WPA (Works Progress Administration), the Tennessee Valley Authority, and the National Recovery Act. And that was just in his first one hundred days!

My father was a passionate Roosevelt fan, although the

National Recovery Act really tested his devotion. At the time he owned a hot-dog restaurant in Allentown, Pennsylvania, called the Orpheum Wiener House. He just couldn't fathom a law that required him to pay a waitress the minimum wage and guarantee her forty hours of work when there was no business. It didn't make sense to him. But even though my father sacrificed plenty under Roosevelt, he kept voting for the guy. In those days, sacrifice wasn't such a maligned concept.

Harry Truman made a huge impression on me because he told it like it was. By the time he was President, I was old enough to know that this was a rare quality, in both politics and business. People were always trying to teach me to keep my mouth shut and be *diplomatic,* and I never did too well on that score. I enjoyed having a President in the Oval Office who spoke his mind in plain English.

Truman was the embodiment of a leader who emerged in a crisis. Nobody thought that little haberdasher from Missouri could fill the great FDR's shoes. But Harry Truman stood ten feet tall. I think we should all pause for a moment to reflect on how lucky we were to have such a practical man of action in the White House when the future of the planet hung in the balance. Thank God Harry Truman wasn't an ideologue.

My second two choices for world leadership are more recent, and I knew both of them quite well. They're Ronald Reagan and Bill Clinton.

Reagan and Clinton have more in common than you'd think. They both lived through rough childhoods, so you can see that their leadership qualities were formed in times of crisis. A lot of people who grow up in homes where there's alcoholism, divorce, and poverty end up with chips on their shoulders. Reagan and Clinton both chose the opposite path. They became optimists. Reagan was the sunniest guy I ever met. He didn't have a mean bone in his body. It was the key to his charisma, and I think that's why they called him the "Great Communicator." He honestly liked people, and his warmth was genuine. I got a dose of it myself. When Reagan heard that my wife Mary was dying, he made a point of calling me to offer comfort and prayers. It was a very low moment for me, and I'll never forget his kindness.

Reagan had strong convictions and the courage to pursue them. He decided that he was going to end the cold war, but he didn't try to go it alone. He put together the team that could do it—and it was *some* team—Reagan, Margaret Thatcher, and Mikhail Gorbachev.

Bill Clinton is also a communicator. In fact, the guy will talk you into the ground. You ask him the time and he'll build you a watch. He loves to talk, but most of the time he makes pretty good sense.

I know there are a lot of people in this country who just can't understand why Clinton was such a popular President, and why he's *still* so popular today. I think it's his passion for governing, his openness, and his respect for people from all countries and all walks of life. The guy really seems to care about making a difference, and that's been even more evident since he left office. There are very few places in the world where Bill Clinton isn't welcomed by throngs of people. These days when he gives a speech, you can see the people in the audience leaning toward him in a way that kind of reminds you of a thirsty man crawling toward an oasis. They're dying for intelligent analysis, but mostly they're dying for words of hope, not fear. "Much has changed in the last fifteen years," Clinton said recently. "But what has not changed is the relentless search for the common good." Those are words that inspire.

Clinton has some pretty good advice for the current administration, if it cares to listen. He said recently, "It's just plain crazy to stop talking to people you disagree with. As long as you keep *talking*, there's hope."

He's right. If you're the leader of the free world, your ideas have to be bigger than your guns.

CAN WE TALK?

Speaking of talking, I wish someone would explain to me why we're still fighting a cold war with Cuba. JFK broke off relations and established a trade embargo against Cuba in 1961, at a time when Fidel Castro's collaboration with the Soviet Union presented a real threat to our shores. But does anyone honestly believe that Cuba poses any threat whatsoever in 2007? The Soviet Union doesn't even *exist* anymore. And we're trading with *China* — and the last time I looked, the Communists were still running that country.

In the final year of Clinton's presidency it looked as though we might stop our saber-rattling. Congress passed the Trade Sanctions Reform and Export Enhancement Act in 2000. The bill cracked the door open a bit for limited, one-way trade. Since then Cuba has bought over half a billion dollars' worth of goods — everything from Vermont cattle to Louisiana rice to

Washington State apples. But we're barred from buying Havana cigars from them, and that really rubs me the wrong way.

But the Bush administration has tried to turn back the clock. Why? Is it because Castro is an evil Communist? Come on—get *real*. The reason we haven't opened the doors to Cuba is because an anti-Castro gang in Miami has held Florida's electoral votes hostage for over forty years. And they've held Florida's elected officials hostage, too—including the President's brother Jeb, who owed his two terms as governor to the former Batista party exiles. They live for the day when their wealth and power will be restored in Cuba, and politicians who pander to that dream tend to do very well in Florida.

The anti-Castro rhetoric sounds more and more ridiculous every year. The right thing to do—the *moral* thing to do—is to start talking. You'd think we would have learned by now that exclusion from opportunity doesn't build democracy.

About thirteen years ago, I was asked to accompany a couple of French businessmen on a trip to Havana. They were good friends of Castro's because they did a huge chicken export business with Cuba, and still do. (Eat your hearts out, American chicken farmers!) They asked me if I'd like to go along. Castro had said he wanted to meet me.

"Geez," I said, "is that legal?" I thought I'd better check, so I called President Clinton's chief of staff, Mac McClarty. I'd been friendly with Mac for years because his father had been my Ford dealer in Hope, Arkansas.

"You can go," Mac told me. "Just don't spend any money there. It's against the law."

The Frenchmen had their own jet, a Falcon, and one of

them was a pilot. When my friends picked me up in California, their plane was loaded with food from Provence—chickens, hams, pastries, bread, cheeses. There was hardly room for my bag, or me.

I'd been to Havana a few times as a young single man. Went to the Tropicana. Saw Carmen Miranda. Smoked cigars. Raised hell. I had fond memories of my times there. But as we drove through Havana in 1994, the old playground looked a little shabby. There weren't that many cars on the road, and most of them were clunkers from Russia or old Fords and Chevys that dated back to the pre-Kennedy era. But the Tropicana was still going strong. Havana's nightlife and gorgeous beaches still attracted tourists from all over the world—except the U.S.

Castro seemed pleased to have this American car guy visiting, and the whole time I was there he treated me like royalty. He told me he'd read both my books. Frankly, I liked the guy. He was well read and as sharp as a tack. He explained that he'd had lots of time to read in jail.

Castro asked me, "When were you last here?" I told him in the final year of Batista's rule.

He laughed dismissively. "Oh, yes, you mean when Cuba was America's speakeasy. It was all being run out of Miami, with Meyer Lansky and his gang. Drugs, gambling, prostitution, corruption. That is why we needed a revolution."

Castro was a good host, and he arranged a couple of excursions. The most memorable was a pigeon-hunting trip. We were awakened at five A.M. one morning, given camouflage uniforms, and asked to assemble in the dining room for a five-thirty A.M. breakfast. I wondered for a moment, *Are we being recruited for Castro's army?*

Surprise! At breakfast we were informed that we were going on a pigeon shoot. Our destination was a sparsely inhabited island, well known for its huge influx of pigeons. Castro apologized that he couldn't accompany us, but he sent his younger brother Raúl (now the acting President of Cuba) to see us off, and his top general accompanied us. At six A.M., we boarded a massive Russian helicopter, which bore the Cuban flag. The helicopter had a crew of six, which included two stewards, two pilots, and two copilots. It was the biggest helicopter I'd ever seen. It was more like a troop carrier!

When I expressed my amazement, Raúl smiled and said, "This is a great helicopter, but we have a very difficult time getting spare parts from Russia anymore."

That made me a little nervous. During the flight, my mind was on prayers, not pigeons.

Castro also threw a dinner in my honor, and I was surprised to see that our own food was served to us at the dinner. The basic French staples, such as caviar, foie gras, and champagne are hard to come by in Cuba. I sat across from Castro, and he regaled us with stories. We had an interpreter, but he understood a lot of English. I'd never thought of Castro as being a lighthearted guy, but I remember laughing a lot.

As the dinner was ending around eleven P.M., Castro motioned to me and said that he wanted to talk to me alone. I followed him out to a big Mercedes with a driver and we got into the backseat. We took off into the night, and I was thinking, *Holy shit, I'm in a car with Fidel Castro, driving through the dark countryside at breakneck speed.* For all I knew they were kidnapping me. We finally reached his place in the country, and sat down outside on the patio for a talk. We were joined by an extremely beautiful young woman who was our interpreter. A young man stood to the side. I wasn't sure if he was a guard, an aide, or the cigar valet. Every time my cigar went out, he'd rush forward and give me a fresh one. Castro explained that you *never* relight a cigar. When it goes out, you throw it away. I told him, "Easy for you to say. You own the factory."

Castro no longer smoked cigars. He told me that after the UN gave him an award for saying that tobacco wasn't healthy he'd felt he had to quit to set a good personal example. "Don't you ever cheat?" I asked, a little amazed. He assured me he did not cheat.

The Cohibas I was smoking were his personal brand. They were short and thick Robustos. "You Americans like long, Panatella-type cigars," Castro said. "Don't you know that sucking in all that air through a super-long cigar is bad for your health?"

What did Castro want to talk about? Politics and business. What else? The guy was hungry for intelligent conversation about the state of the world.

It was obvious he was pissed off at the Soviets. They'd screwed him. They'd left him to twist in the wind. It was lonely being one of the only Communist countries left in the world. But Castro had some very interesting observations about the transition from Communism to the free market. In his opinion, the Soviet Union went about the process backward, but China was getting it right.

"Gorbachev did it wrong," he told me. "The Soviets should have done the economics first and then thrown out the commissars. Now Russia has nothing but corruption and chaos. In China the Communists still have a strong hold. They are maintaining power while they gradually transition to open markets."

"You're talking like a bloody capitalist, Fidel," I said. "You're saying, fix the economy first, and the social order will follow."

Castro was a very provocative guy. "Do you want to bring democracy here, or do you want to bring some of your prosperity?" he asked. "Tell me how to do the last one. I don't want to hear about the first one."

What could I say? *Yeah, but you're a dictator? If people get in your way you can knock them off?* I kept *that* thought to myself, but I didn't believe a prosperous, free market could coexist with a dictatorship.

"Didn't you pick the wrong side?" I asked.

He said maybe, but the revolution kind of got out of hand.

"Well, what did you expect from the revolution?"

"I didn't expect it to be so easy," he said.

I didn't want to overstep my bounds, but I was curious. "Fidel, I've been here a couple of days now, and I visited the sights. I see your picture in all the offices and on all the buildings. But it always looks to me like Che Guevara's picture is above yours—and it's bigger than yours."

Castro shrugged. "To the young people, he is like a cult hero. A born revolutionary."

"You knew Che well," I said. "You were close to him. Can I ask you a question?"

He nodded.

"Why did Che go to Bolivia? To export revolution, right?"

Another nod.

"And as soon as he got there he was assassinated. Did you have anything to do with that?"

I suppose Castro was surprised at my boldness. Hell, *I* was surprised at my boldness. "Lee," he said, "we've been talking openly, but if you're interested in that kind of thing, why don't you check with your own CIA?"

We talked until two-thirty in the morning, and I enjoyed it. I thought we'd made a real connection.

As we left Cuba, with a supply of Cohiba cigars (a *gift*) packed in my bag, I hoped it wouldn't be my last visit. When I got back to the United States, I called McClarty. "Mac," I said, "Castro is ready to talk."

"Maybe he brainwashed you," Mac said.

"No," I said, "he leveled with me. Look, our policy is hurting young kids and old people. It's doing a lot of damage — over what? Ideology?"

I was so frustrated that for a while after my visit I thought I might volunteer for the job of unofficial diplomat to Cuba. But no one was interested. And thirteen years after my visit, we're *still* not talking. What a missed opportunity! What is it going to take to convince our leaders that the road forward starts with a conversation?

A TIP FROM DALE CARNEGIE

Ever since I took the Dale Carnegie course when I was twenty-five, I've kept his book *How to Win Friends and Influence People* on the shelf. I still have my original copy, and it's pretty tattered.

I must have referred to it hundreds of times in my life. Do you know what Dale Carnegie's first rule was? "If you want to gather honey, don't kick over the beehive." That's pure common sense—something we are often lacking these days.

Dale Carnegie also had some good advice about being a leader, and he made a point of saying that it applied to presidents and kings as well as to ordinary businesspeople. Although he wrote *How to Win Friends and Influence People* seventy years ago, Carnegie's principles are just as relevant today.

Sometimes we forget that government officials and heads of nations are human beings. The greatest impediment to getting along is having preconceived notions that someone is all-holy, all-evil, or made of stone or steel. In my life I've been amazed by how often my negative ideas about people are proven wrong when I actually meet them. For instance, in 2005, when I was invited to a dinner party hosted by Prince Charles and his bride-to-be Camilla at Highgrove, the prince's personal residence, I was *sure* I knew what they'd be like—very stiff and proper. I got ready for a dull evening of protocol and pomp. Was I ever wrong! Camilla greeted us at the door with a warm smile, and insisted, "Please call me Camilla." Charles was relaxed and talkative. They both had great senses of humor. It was one of the most enjoyable evenings I'd had in a long time.

The point is, people are people. Even the mighty have feelings and pride. Just like everyone else, they appreciate a pat on the back or a way to save face when they've dug a hole for themselves. When it comes right down to it, being a leader in the world is just a matter of winning friends and influencing people with a spirit of hope.

VII

Meet the coalition
of the UNwilling

I may be getting old, but there's nothing wrong with my memory or my attention span—at least not yet. The folks from the
Bush administration would like us to forget that we went to war
in Iraq because they falsely claimed Saddam Hussein had
weapons of mass destruction. They'd like us to forget their
phony campaign to connect Saddam Hussein to 9/11, so they
could do what they'd wanted to do all along. If I live to be a hundred (which I hope to do), I'll never understand how we got so
duped.

We went to war on a lie. Congress didn't debate it. The
press didn't challenge it. It got trumped up in secret meetings.
The generals weren't allowed in the room. Secretary of State
Colin Powell even got fooled. And now that we've made a mess
of things, the only way out is to start telling the truth.

The generals finally came forward to do just that, although
it took them three years. If anyone doubts how much trouble

we're in, just listen to the generals. They say that the *rhetoric* of the White House hasn't been matched by either *resources* or *resolve*. The drumbeats have drowned out common sense. They say we are bankrupt in leadership.

Iraq is a war nobody wanted—unless you count Iran, who has watched us accomplish what *their* eight-year war with Iraq could not. Unless you count the Taliban in Afghanistan, whose narcotics trade is thriving. George Bush says our enemies "hate us for our freedom." They really hate us for our arrogance. But they *love* it when we get stupid. And, folks, we've been stupid. Big time.

THE LESSONS OF HISTORY

One of the qualities that made Winston Churchill a great leader was his historical imagination. "The longer you look back," he wrote, "the farther you can look forward." He once complained to a friend, "We live in the most thoughtless of ages. Every day headlines and short views. I have tried to drag history up a little nearer to our own times in case it should be a guide in present difficulties." Good idea!

The war in Iraq is a failure of historical imagination. Didn't we learn any lessons from Vietnam? Vietnam was also a failure of historical imagination, which showed that we learned nothing from Korea.

Many years ago, Joseph Califano, who was a member of Lyndon Johnson's and later Jimmy Carter's administration, told me this story. It was right after Johnson had been elected in 1964, and Johnson and Califano went to visit General Douglas MacArthur, who was retired and living in the Waldorf Towers in New York City. MacArthur said to Johnson, "Sonny, never get involved in a land war in Asia." When they left his apartment, Johnson was furious. "Did you hear that?" he asked Califano. "The son of a bitch called me Sonny. I'm the President of the United States, and he called me Sonny!" He couldn't get over it. Unfortunately, Johnson missed the real message—the one about the ground war in Asia. Kennedy missed it, too, because I understand that MacArthur told him the same thing. I wonder if he called JFK *Sonny*.

When the Bush administration said we would be greeted as liberators, I knew right away we were in trouble. The lessons of history would have told a different story, but history was never consulted.

TRAGIC CONSEQUENCES

When I talk to John Murtha, he says he feels personally betrayed. In his heart Murtha is still a marine. You never stop being a marine. He feels responsible for the guys we've placed in peril without a plan for winning. Murtha spends his weekends visiting the wounded at Walter Reed Army Medical Center in Washington, D.C. He describes their injuries as *horrible*. Those who survive roadside bombings—the most common injury— usually have massive head injuries and loss of limbs. Their families are crying, *begging* Murtha to do something. They believe their kids have become nothing more than targets, driving around in poorly armored Humvees and getting blown up. For *what*?

Have you noticed that we never hear much about the wounded? The media keeps a running count of the dead, but why not the wounded? Where do you even *find out* how many have been wounded? Let me tell you something. It's not easy. The Pentagon doesn't publish that information unless it is specifically requested by the media. Why do you think *that* is? Could it be because the number is so *big*? I challenge the media to do just that. Put the number in bold print, right next to the number for those killed. (For your information, the official number of Americans wounded in action in Iraq is currently around 24,000, but that doesn't account for thousands of non-combat injuries.)

And where is Bush, the Commander in Chief? For a guy who loves photo ops so much, there's one photo op you never see: the President in Dover, Delaware, standing next to a flag-draped coffin. He doesn't want to be identified with coffins. For the first time in memory, cameras have been banned from Dover. The coffins arrive in the deep of night, when nobody can see them. Hell, they don't even *call* them coffins. They call them "transfer tubes."

IS IT REALLY WORTH IT?

The cost of human life is the greatest tragedy of Iraq, but don't forget the other costs. Let's look at it from the perspective of a CEO. When you decide to launch a project—whether you're building a car or starting a war—one of the first things you do is look at the cost/benefit picture. That is, what are we *getting* for the money?

As of this writing, the cost of the war is estimated at about half a trillion dollars. But according to some experts, the true cost could be as high as $2 trillion, when you factor in lifetime disability and health care for the wounded, the interest on our debt, and the rising oil prices.

On the ground, it's been kind of hard to keep track of how much we're spending, because the accounting is extremely loose in the new Iraq. It's like the Wild West over there. At one point, $1.5 billion was floating around in cash, to be used to hire workers and pay off mullahs, and God knows what else. Paul Bremer, who was in charge of the rebuilding effort for a while, kept $600 million in *cash* on hand. I guess he put it in his sock drawer.

Don't forget. That's *your* money they're spending. Do you want to throw it into an Iraqi sinkhole, or do you want to provide health care? Do you want to hand it over to Halliburton, or do you want to make sure American kids go to college?

To give you an idea of the magnitude of the amount we're pouring into Iraq, let's look at the conservative estimate of what half a trillion dollars would buy here at home:

- We could hire 8 MILLION SCHOOLTEACHERS.
- We could give FREE HEALTH CARE to everyone for one year.
- We could provide 25 MILLION COLLEGE SCHOL- ARSHIPS.

- We could give every American FREE GAS for one year.
- We could build 3 MILLION AFFORDABLE HOUS-ING UNITS.
- We could hire 8 MILLION POLICE, FIRE, AND EMT WORKERS.

We could put a dent in some of the most pervasive problems we face as a nation. So, the next time someone in government says we can't afford health care or education or border security, just remember, it's all about *priorities.*

FACTS ARE STUBBORN THINGS

Ronald Reagan once said, "Facts are stubborn things." He actually got that quote from John Adams. The Bush administration doesn't really believe in facts. It believes if you tell a lie often enough it becomes true. But those inconvenient facts keep getting in the way. They said there were weapons of mass destruction. There were none. They said the war would take six months tops. It's been four years. They said Saddam Hussein colluded with Al Qaeda on the 9/11 attacks. That never happened.

I could go on, but the lies get boring. The administration likes to call their mistakes "faulty intelligence." There was no faulty intelligence. Let's call a lie a lie. Can't we believe *anything* these guys say?

It takes courage to face the truth, but I believe we must. Not only about the disastrous course of the war, but about our nation's mixed history with Saddam Hussein's regime. Don't forget that we *backed* Saddam in his war with Iran. (There's a famous photograph from 1983 that shows Donald Rumsfeld shaking Saddam Hussein's hand. Everyone is smiling!) The Reagan and George H. W. Bush administrations provided Iraq with over $15 billion in loan guarantees. When Saddam sprayed chemical gas on the Kurds, he used *U.S. helicopters* sold to him for crop dusting. With Saddam now in his grave, the whole truth may never be told. But one thing is clear: Nobody's hands are clean in this one—especially not ours.

THE COALITION OF THE DWINDLING

Can you call it a coalition when it's just you and one other guy? Let's compare Bush senior's coalition in 1990 with his son's. The phrase "go it alone" takes on new meaning with Bush junior.

In March 2003, as we were gearing up for war, the White House published a list of forty-eight nations that were participating in the Coalition of the Willing. Forty-eight seems like a big number, until you look at the list and the troops numbers. Most of them contributed fewer than a hundred soldiers. Now, even that coalition has become the Coalition of the Dwindling. We're down to twenty-three nations, totaling less than fifteen thousand troops—half of those from Great Britain. And the dwindling continues. Here's the *real* picture (as of this writing):

United States:	140,000 troops
Great Britain:	7,200 troops
All others:	7,000 troops

You might call that a coalition. I call it an American war.

If you want an example of what an actual coalition looks like, take a look at the Persian Gulf war. Bush's daddy had it right:

United States:	550,000 troops
Saudi Arabia:	118,000 troops
Turkey:	100,000 troops
Great Britain:	43,000 troops
Egypt:	40,000 troops
United Arab Emirates:	40,000 troops
Oman:	25,500 troops
France:	18,000 troops
Other nations:	40,000 troops

One thing you notice right away—in addition to the sheer numbers—is that the gulf war coalition drew its strength largely from the Arab world. They were our allies. Name one Arab nation that signed on for the current Iraqi war. Instead of bringing the Arab world together, the war has sparked a rise in violence across the region, our intelligence agencies report. The best recruiting tool for the jihadists is the war in Iraq.

DOESN'T ANYBODY HAVE A PLAN?

Bush and company had a fantasy that we could bring democracy to Iraq and it would cause a domino effect in the Middle East. Suddenly every Arab nation would embrace democracy. What were they *smoking*?

Condi Rice said the problems are "the birth pangs of a new Middle East." Well, it's an awfully long time to be in labor.

Today, they don't even talk about establishing democracy anymore. Mostly they talk about how we can pull our finger out of the dike without causing a tsunami.

The war in Iraq has already exceeded World War II in the length of the conflict. Where's the plan?

After the 2006 election, Bush fired Secretary of Defense Donald Rumsfeld, but you have to wonder if it was in recognition of the mess we were in or just political expediency. How many *fired* people do you know who are given elaborate ceremonies praising their years of service?

Before he left office, Rumsfeld leaked the contents of a memo he'd sent the President several weeks earlier, perhaps anticipating the need to shore up his legacy. In the memo he called for a new direction, then gave a laundry list of alternatives. It was too little, too late.

The long-awaited report of the Iraq Study Group, led by Bush senior's old pal James Baker, left the President with the choice of embracing it and admitting failure, or ignoring it and doing nothing. Can you guess which he chose? This is a President incapable of admitting failure.

Let's apply some common sense here. If the head of a car company was losing money like crazy on its latest model, you wouldn't hear the CEO say, "The solution is to build more cars. We have to support our investment." Not if he wanted to keep his job. He'd better have a new plan — and I mean *now*.

Remember Colin Powell's Pottery Barn rule, "You break it, you own it"? Boy, that's pretty bad news. The way things are going in Iraq these days, we own a pile of crockery. There is no electricity, no infrastructure, no security for citizens, the government is a joke. What there seems to be plenty of is *violence*. I heard there was an update on the Pottery Barn rule: "*We* broke it, *you* own it."

Let's face it. Even if the war itself was started under false pretenses, we could have achieved tremendous good will and positive results if we'd been prepared for the aftermath of the invasion. Instead, we sent a bunch of Republican Party hacks over to build a nation. In many cases, their only credentials were loyalty to the President. They didn't have to speak the language, know anything about the Middle East, or have any experience with the nuts and bolts of nation building. You can talk all you want about the promise of democracy in Iraq, but you can't really have a democracy if you're afraid to leave your house. And democracy can't be planted in a field of civil war.

OSAMA BIN FORGOTTEN

After 9/11, Bush was determined to catch Osama bin Laden and bring him to justice. "There's an old poster out west," our cowboy leader said, "'Wanted: Dead or Alive.'" Now, *that*'s a mission the American people could really get behind. But Bush pulled nearly all of our troops out of Afghanistan and sent them to Iraq, without capturing bin Laden. The 9/11 mastermind is still on the loose. Well, I'll tell you *one* place Osama is NOT hiding: in *Iraq*.

In July 2006 the secret unit assigned to track down bin Laden was disbanded. In September Bush told a reporter that capturing bin Laden was not a priority. That boggles my mind. The guy who is responsible for 9/11 is NOT a priority. The guy who "tried to kill my daddy" IS a priority. It makes you wonder if Bush ever intended to capture Osama bin Laden after all. It adds to the evidence that we're not really fighting the *War on Terror* in Iraq. We're fighting to survive a civil war that *we* enabled. Call me paranoid, but I'm starting to think that whenever a Saudi is involved—even if it's bin Laden himself—we just aren't that motivated.

Jay Leno joked about it, but it's really not so funny. When there were rumors (later discredited) that bin Laden was dead, Leno quipped that officials in Saudi Arabia believed them. "The reason they think he's dead," Leno said, "is that the checks they send him keep coming back."

LET'S DO OUR FRIENDS A FAVOR

Which brings me to my proposal. If our goal is to spread democracy throughout the Middle East, why don't we do our friends a favor and call for a regime change in Saudi Arabia? Why don't we bring *them* democracy? If it's good enough for Iraq, it's good enough for Saudi Arabia.

It makes sense. In all the years that the Saudis have been tight with the Bushes, wouldn't you think some of that love of freedom would have rubbed off on them? Why do you suppose we've left their brutal little theocracy alone? If democracy in the Middle East was such a big deal, why did we start with a bitter enemy, before we offered it to our very best friend?

The Bush family's ties to Saudi Arabia are well documented. I saw it for myself on a visit to former Saudi ambassador Prince Bandar's mansion in Aspen, Colorado. The prince had quite a luxurious spread near America's favorite ski slope. He took me on a tour of the property, and pointed out two bungalows. One was named for Bush senior and one was named for Bush junior.

This may explain the fact that even though Saudi Arabia had its fingerprints all over 9/11, the Bush administration refused to demand accountability. Saudi Arabia got a pass when Bush was looking for countries that harbored terrorists. Saudi Arabia got a pass when it was discovered that millions of dollars had flowed from the Saudis to Al Qaeda. Saudi Arabia even got a pass on the fifteen Saudi hijackers. Imagine how the Bush administration would have spun it if even *one* of the 9/11 hijackers had been from Iraq. It takes a lot of balls to ignore the fifteen hijackers that were from Saudi Arabia.

Thanks to the reliable Bush family consigliere James Baker, whose firm successfully represented the Saudi government in a $1 trillion lawsuit brought by the 9/11 families, Saudi Arabia was declared blameless. I guess that's what *friends* are for.

So, back to the question: Why don't we bring democracy to our friends the Saudis? This theocracy is opposed to everything we stand for. If you were going to name an axis of evil, you could easily start in Saudi Arabia. It's an absolute monarchy, where all the decisions are made by the King. There is no constitution. No legislature. No due process. It is illegal to demonstrate against the government. It is illegal to practice any religion but Islam. Corporal punishment is still practiced. (That means if you steal a loaf of bread, they cut off your hand.) Public executions are regularly held. Women are not allowed to vote. Women must have written permission from a man to study, work, or travel. The religious police are everywhere, making sure that women are covered, that women aren't driving cars, that everyone is toeing the line. These religious police are no better than the Taliban—and let me tell you, they're scary. Once I was at the Riyadh Hilton with a group of top U.S. executives. We were on a tour of nations, sponsored by *Time* magazine. The cameraman had a knapsack supposedly full of film canisters, but it actually held dozens of miniature bottles of liquor. He slipped a tiny bottle of scotch into a paper bag, and gave it to me to enjoy in my room. The wife of the American ambassador saw me standing in the hall chatting and holding my little paper bag. She whispered to me, "Better get rid of that. If they find alcohol on you in a public place, they will lock you up tonight, no questions asked, and we will not be able to help you." I couldn't drink that bottle fast enough!

Saudi Arabia is one of the poorest countries in the Middle East, with its vast oil wealth being squandered by the few. The excess is mind-boggling. Hundreds of gold-encased palaces, hundreds of wives, millions blown on vacations, gambling, high living. These guys make Saddam Hussein look downright middle-class. Outside the palace gates, ordinary Saudis face high unemployment, a crumbling infrastructure, and a grim future.

To top it off, every schoolchild in Saudi Arabia is taught that their *sole* duty in life is to destroy everything America stands for. With friends like these, you don't need enemies. Why do we tolerate it with a smile?

The answer is simple: It's the *oil*. We have sold our soul for oil. And if that doesn't piss you off, nothing will. Our troops are being blown up in the Middle East so we can bring democracy to Iraq, while we're in bed with a regime that would sooner see us wiped off the face of the earth. The only possible explanation is oil.

VIII

What will we do
for oil?

When are we going to stop denying that the energy policy of the United States is run by the oil cartel? Oil is behind the war in Iraq. Oil is the reason we give the fundamentalist, terrorist-breeding theocracy of Saudi Arabia a pass. Oil is the reason we can't get a goddamn energy policy in this country. Almost every important administration official has a connection to the oil industry.

You may be thinking, "Lee's going soft. Now that he's not building cars, he's becoming antioil." But this isn't about being antioil. It's about taking an honest look at what our oil connections are doing to us. We'd better get our heads out of the Arabian sand and start facing some facts.

Can anyone tell me what our long-term energy policy is? I've been trying to figure that out, and I keep coming back to *oil*. Is our only energy policy to open up new drilling sites for oil? I don't know. Maybe we should ask Dick Cheney.

Before I die, I want to read the notes from Vice President Cheney's energy task force. Remember that one? Cheney convened his secret task force within ten days of taking office back in 2001. Who participated? What was discussed? What evidence was outlined? What options were studied?

Oh, you can't ask that. Those details were *private*. It was a matter of *executive privilege*. That was Cheney's position when Congress wanted to take a look at the process. This administration loves executive privilege. They define it as "we can do whatever we want." Cheney went on to fight every effort for scrutiny all the way to the Supreme Court, where his duck-hunting pal Justice Antonin Scalia supported his position.

Well, even without the details it didn't take a genius to figure out that the meetings had a certain tilt. All you had to do was read the task force's recommendations. Oil, oil, and more oil. According to Cheney's group, the energy priority of the Bush administration was to lift sanctions against oil-producing countries like Iran, Syria, and Iraq, so that American companies could take advantage of the plentiful opportunities for oil exploration.

To this day, we don't know what actually transpired in those meetings. However, we now know who attended them. Six of the meetings were held with Enron executives. Others included representatives from ExxonMobil, Conoco, Shell, BP, and various utility companies. Chevron executives didn't attend, but sent written recommendations, which, in some cases, were adopted verbatim.

What about the environmentalists, the alternative-energy companies, the scientists? They were lumped into one meeting at the very end of the process. To show how interested he was in energy alternatives, Cheney even paraded the solar and wind people out for a Rose Garden photo op—the day before the report was released. There were no Rose Garden photo ops for the oil execs. I guess they were just a little camera shy.

Over the years, bits and pieces of information have dribbled out about the task force, including its preoccupation with Iraqi oil. Documents released in 2003 include a map of Iraqi oil fields, pipelines, refineries, and terminals, as well as a chart detailing Iraqi oil and gas projects, and one titled "Foreign Suitors for Iraqi Oil Field Contracts." So, in early 2001, the oilmen inside and outside the White House were already dreaming of a post-Saddam oil bonanza.

Like I said, before I die I want to read the minutes of those meetings. In the meantime, it's really not that hard to connect the dots.

THE FRIENDS HE KEEPS

You can tell a lot about a person by looking at who his friends are. Bush feels comfortable around certain types who share his worldview—especially those who look at the world through oil-tinted glasses. There's Dick Cheney, of course. The former Halliburton CEO brings the oil industry to the head table. But there are others.

A lot of people probably don't realize that Secretary of State Condi Rice first came to Bush's attention when she was serving on the board of directors of Chevron. The oilmen loved Condi so much during her ten-year stint on the board that they named an oil tanker after her. (It was quietly renamed when she joined the Bush administration.)

Then there's Don Evans, an old buddy from the gas and oil business, who became commerce secretary in the first term. And Lawrence Lindsey, Bush's former chief economic advisor, previously of the Enron Advisory Board. And don't forget James Baker, the Carlyle Group honcho, whose firm represents oil companies, defense contractors, AND the Saudi royal family. Bush may not *love* Uncle Jim, but without his help he might not even be in the White House. Baker rode to the rescue during the Florida recount debacle in 2000, and saved Bush's presidency. He tried to save it again in 2006 by heading up the Iraq Study Group, but that didn't turn out so well.

Do you know who the secretary of energy is? Probably not. But if you're keeping track, it's a guy named Samuel Bodman. In the private sector he was a chemical engineer and an investment banker. Bush's kind of people.

IS IT GETTING HOT IN HERE?

In his 2006 State of the Union address, Bush said, "America is addicted to oil." You want to yell, "It just *hit* you that we're addicted to oil?" An oilman accusing the American people of being "addicted to oil" is like a drug dealer accusing junkies of being addicted to drugs.

What is this administration doing to help us break our addiction? Well, it started by presenting a budget that cuts spending for projects that improve energy efficiency. And its blind determination to ignore the environmental consequences of our energy expenditure is sheer lunacy. In spite of the unequivocal report by the Intergovernmental Panel on Climate Change in February 2007, the Bush administration has continued to suggest that the jury is still out on global warming. What jury is that—the O.J. *jury*? The facts are getting pretty hard to ignore.

Since I spent my life in an industry that helped pollute the environment, it's probably no surprise that I came late to enlightenment on this subject. One of the reasons I didn't support Al Gore for President in 2000 was that I thought he was a little nuts on the subject of global warming. But then I saw Gore's movie, *An Inconvenient Truth*. I never thought I'd pay eight dollars to watch a PowerPoint presentation given by Al Gore, but I have to say it opened my eyes. The glaciers are melting, the sea levels are rising, and it's all happening soon, like in the next twenty-five to fifty years. It reminds me of Bill Cosby's old routine on Noah. When Noah ignored God's command that he build an ark, God boomed, *"How long can you tread water?"*

As I thought about it, I realized that I didn't really need to see Gore's movie to know that something was off-kilter with the climate. During a trip to Boston in December 2006, I found everyone walking around in light sweaters, enjoying temperatures in the sixties. Who could complain—right? To tell you the truth, I was a little nervous about the price we might be paying for the balmy weather. Then in February 2007, the Midwest and Northeast got slammed with record snowfalls (over 100 inches in some places) and ice storms. These weather extremes are a warning. Who's listening?

SHOWING LEADERSHIP ON ENERGY

It's the job of a leader to make tough decisions—to look ahead and say, "What can we do *right now* to help solve the energy crisis?" There just *has* to be more to a long-term energy strategy than finding ways to get our hands on additional oil. We've got to take the long view. Will the oil that currently exists on this planet—including that which remains undiscovered—supply the earth for the next one hundred years? How about the next one thousand years? With the rapid development in China and India, demand for oil and gas is doubling right now. Even if there were enough oil, it isn't going to come from our own shores, which means we'll continue to be dependent on foreign oil. And when you're dependent on people whose goal in life is to wipe you out, that's a pretty sorry state of affairs.

So, we have to get creative. Start thinking about another way of approaching the energy problem. If I were in charge of energy, my policy would go something like this:

1. **I'd ask for sacrifice.** I'll admit that I spent nearly fifty years convincing people to buy more cars, but maybe it's time to take another look at that. During my time in the auto industry the average family went from one car to two cars, and in some cases three cars. And that doesn't even count the huge car rental industry. Americans love the convenience of being able to get up and go whenever they want and with whoever they want. The carpool lanes haven't really worked so well. People

don't like to ride-share. But what if people carpooled two days a week? Or even *one* day a week. Surely we can take a *little bit* of sacrifice, can't we?

We're a nation at war. Why can't our Commander in Chief call for sacrifice? During World War II, people grew their own vegetables, saved tinfoil, *and* submitted to gas rationing without complaint. Where's the spirit of national purpose?

2. **I'd push for a gas tax.** When Ronald Reagan was President, and my friend Tip O'Neill was Speaker of the House, I proposed to them that we could dramatically cut the deficit if we increased the gas tax by fifty cents a gallon. I figured we could raise $50 billion just like that. Reagan laughed. He said, "Lee, you're a smart guy, but my pollster tells me I'd commit political suicide if I raised the gas tax. You know why? Because once a week when they were filling up their tanks, people would be reminded that *I* raised their taxes." He added, just in case I didn't get the point, "That's why *you're* sitting on that side of the desk, and *I'm* the President."

Nobody ever wants to raise taxes, especially on gas. But we're *already* paying tax every time they spike the price at the pump. The only difference is, we're paying it to the *oil cartel*, not to ourselves. And don't kid yourselves. Some of this money is being turned into weapons to fight *our* troops.

If you look at the world at large, we're behind the eight ball when it comes to taxing and using gas. The United States has the cheapest gas in the world because of our low gas taxes, which, combining federal and state taxes, average about forty-seven cents per gallon. In Great Britain, the tax is around $4.25 per gallon. In Germany, France, and Italy, the tax is close to $4. Now, remember, the tax is on top of the price of gas. So, when I was in Italy in the fall of 2006, we paid a whopping $6.70 for a gallon of gas. Can you imagine the howls in the United States if we had to pay anything *close* to that price? The Italians didn't seem so upset about it. Maybe that's because they're driving fuel-efficient cars, and they don't drive as much as we do.

3. **I'd use the gas tax to develop alternatives.** Let's have an Energy Summit to explore the development and use of alternatives — solar power, wind power, electricity, ethanol, natural gas, biodiesel, and others. We might have to wait until Cheney and his friends are out of office. Don't want to risk another energy task force. But then we should get aggressive.

   Another obvious way to free up a few bucks for research and development would be to take it out of the hides of the grossly overpaid oil executives. Last year the chief executives of the five largest oil companies earned almost *a billion dollars* in compensation. Imagine what that kind of money could buy if it were invested in research and development. I hope that's something the new Democratic majority sinks its teeth into.

4. **I'd break the oil cartel.** If we want to stand for something in the Middle East, we should forget about establishing democracy, and pressure our friends and

enemies alike to get rid of the oil cartel. The way it works now, we have no control over the price or distribution of oil. Is that acceptable? OPEC, which has been around for thirty-six years, controls the oil spigot at the whim of the cartel, and we've all been suckered in. I'm not naïve that it will be easy to break the cartel, but right now we're not even *trying*. What's the best way to start? Bring down the demand by vigorously exploring alternative energy sources.

5. **I'd demand higher standards from Detroit.** In 1975, after the first Arab oil embargo, our government enacted something called the Corporate Average Fuel Economy (CAFE) standards. These standards have helped to more than double the fuel economy of cars in the last thirty years. There are plans in place to increase CAFE standards on light trucks. The car companies have become pretty good at figuring out ways to increase fuel economy. The technology is there. But we need a higher bar to reach for.

  One way you increase fuel economy is to make cars lighter. Now, I know that people get all hot and bothered about lighter cars. They think they're less safe. Is that true? No. For the most part, safety is a product of design, not weight. Instead of building heavier cars to protect ourselves from other people in heavy cars, let's put the focus on building lighter, more fuel-efficient cars. Even the larger vehicles, like SUVs and minivans, can be built lighter.

6. **I'd consider restoring the nuclear option.** I'd push for

a reactivation of nuclear power as a viable option. It's time to stop running scared from Chernobyl and start realizing that we now have the systems and technology to build fail-safe nuclear power plants. All over the European Union, they're investing in building cleaner, safer nuclear power plants. Europe derives about one third of its electricity from nuclear power. France is the leader, at 78 percent. Even Russia is planning a major expansion of nuclear energy. This renewable source of energy is not only environmentally friendly, it's efficient. Our problem is that when we got worried about nuclear plant safety, we turned it over to the lawyers to fight for safeguards. Here's a tip: Never turn the future of your country over to the lawyers! The Europeans did it right. They turned the problem over to the engineers. The United States is lagging far behind in nuclear energy, when we should be on the leading edge.

Of course, you can't fuel a car with nuclear energy, but you can run a car on electricity generated by nuclear power. In December 2006, I attended the Alternative Energy Show in Los Angeles, and the big news for cars was plug-in hybrids. They were being touted as the wave of the future, and I agree. That will happen much faster if we restore our investment in nuclear power. I can imagine a scene in the not too distant future when one spouse will turn to the other at bedtime and say, "Honey, did you remember to turn off the lights, bring in the cat, and plug in the car?"

7. **I would create a sense of urgency.** Where's the sense of

urgency about solving this problem? There is none. But all you have to do is look at other times in history when we created a national purpose. We did it with the Manhattan Project when we built the A-bomb. We did it with NASA when we went to the moon. Do you mean to tell me that with all our technological genius and know-how, we can't figure out a solution to a problem that is so devastating to our economy and the environment?

We've got options. This isn't an unsolvable problem. I'm here to say that we can tackle this and *win*. And we need some leaders who will show us the way. Let's hear *their* ideas. In the coming campaign, energy should be front and center, and we—the voters—can put it there.

IX

Free trade must be *fair* trade

It was September 1993. I was at my house in Tuscany, where I spend a few weeks every autumn. At about two A.M. the phone rang, waking me out of a sound sleep.

The woman's voice on the other end of the line was wide awake and chipper. "I have the President on the line," she said.

"Okay," I answered, wondering, president of *what*? Then the familiar voice burst over the line. "Lee, it's Bill Clinton."

I sat up a little straighter on the edge of my bed. When the President calls, you listen.

"Listen, Lee, can you come to the White House around ten tomorrow morning? I have something very important to discuss with you."

"Well, Mr. President, I would be happy to, but I'm not sure it's physically possible. You know, I'm in Italy."

"You're in Italy?" He was genuinely surprised. "They didn't tell me that." He paused. "What time is it over there?"

I looked at the clock. "It's just after two in the morning."

He laughed. "Sorry. Go back to sleep. But get here as soon as you can."

A few days later, sitting in the Oval Office, I had to smile as President Clinton attempted to persuade me to join his fight to pass the North American Free Trade Agreement. He especially wanted me to take on Ross Perot, who had launched a loud campaign against the agreement. I have to say it was gutsy of Clinton to call on me. A lot of people said I was a protectionist, but Clinton realized that I'd never been a protectionist. All I'd ever asked for was that trade agreements be *fair*. Show me a plan that's fair and beneficial, and I was on board. The *protectionist* in this debate was Ross Perot, who was appealing to everyone's fears about losing jobs. Ross said we'd hear a "giant sucking sound" of jobs leaving America for Mexico. He was scaring American workers to death about NAFTA. That's where I came in, I guess. Clinton figured I was a credible voice on trade issues. The only thing he had to do was convince *me*.

To a lot of people's surprise—including *mine*—Clinton did sell me on NAFTA. When you think about it, what could make more sense than a trade agreement with our closest neighbors that included a common commitment to resolving environmental and labor issues? The goal of NAFTA was to improve economic, environmental, and trade conditions in Canada, the United States, and Mexico. The improved economic conditions and open markets would generate *more* jobs, not fewer. That was a program I could support, and I helped Clinton sell NAFTA. The bill passed in 1994.

A lot of people have asked me, if I had to do it all over again, would I support NAFTA? While NAFTA has had some positive trade benefits on paper, it's hard to call the agreement a roaring success. The ideal of NAFTA—to set in motion a collaborative process in our corner of the world, where trade would not only be *free*, but also *fair*—was noble enough. But NAFTA has yet to fulfill its goal of attracting other countries to our south, such as Argentina, Brazil, Chile, and, yes, *even* Venezuela. In the long run, that will need to happen to make NAFTA viable. And it's hard to ignore the continued decline of U.S. manufacturing, which hasn't been stemmed by NAFTA.

The big question when it comes to trade is how we acknowledge global realities and move forward, without destroying our competitive edge. Free trade is one of the fundamental principles of our capitalist economy, but America has a bad habit of giving away the store.

FREE TRADE HAS TO BE FAIR TRADE

For more than twenty years, I have been preaching the primary rule of free trade: It must be fair. For the most part, my words have fallen on deaf ears, because the trade imbalance is just getting worse. It's currently at around $800 billion—over *three quarters of a trillion* dollars. That's how much more we're importing than we're exporting. This is happening because the United States has thrown our market wide open to anyone who wants to set up a booth. We worship at the altar of free trade, and it's killing us. At the very least, it's time we started charging admission to the American market. And the price of a ticket has to be a little fairness and reciprocity.

It might interest you to know that President Bush says there's no reason to be alarmed about the trade deficit. He says other countries will always be happy to lend us the money to finance our deficit. Is *this* our trade policy? If so, we are, to quote Bush's father, in *deep doo-doo*. Because the bill will come due, you can bet on it. As the trade imbalance grows, our influence in the world shrinks.

Bush's father took the trade imbalance a *lot* more seriously when he was President. Near the end of his term, I was part of a team accompanying him on a high-profile trip to Japan. Our mission was to urge the Japanese to open up their markets to American products and balance the trade deficit—most of which was accounted for by cars and parts. The previous year American car companies had sold a measly 32,000 cars in Japan, while Japan had sold more than 2.5 *million* cars in America. Furthermore, for all their talk about building plants in the United States and providing jobs for Americans, Japanese car companies were still shipping most of their parts and components from Japan.

We visited a new Toys "R" Us store that had just opened in Osaka. The Japanese were trying to show us how receptive they were to American products. While we toured the store, Bush held up a toy bank in the shape of a Chrysler minivan. "Hey, Lee," he said excitedly, "what do you think of this?"

I stared at the toy and said, "Great. But I thought we were here to talk about the *big* seven-passenger minivans, not the nickel-and-dime kind."

The trip went downhill from there. I flew with the President to Tokyo on *Air Force One*, where we met with Japanese business leaders. Basically, they told us—always politely and with a smile—that the reason more Japanese weren't buying American cars was because our cars were inferior. That was a load of crap.

The reason we weren't selling cars in Japan was that the deck was stacked against us. Japan wasn't practicing free trade. Japan was practicing *predatory* trade, and it still is. This little island with a big ego does everything in its power to keep the trade imbalance great. It doesn't have to bother with the rules of the free enterprise system. The Bank of Tokyo and the Ministry of International Trade and Industry (MITI) make sure that the yen is manipulated (they called it "managed trade") so that it's cheaper for Americans to buy Japanese cars and more expensive for the Japanese to buy American cars.

Bush senior's mission to Japan didn't go well—to say the least. It didn't help that Bush ended the trip by vomiting on the Prime Minister at a state dinner. On our way home, we stopped for fuel in Anchorage. I went inside the building, and there was a TV on the wall, tuned into Johnny Carson. I walked in just in time to hear Carson joke, "If you had to eat raw fish, and sit across from Lee Iacocca, you'd throw up, too."

THE NEW PLAYERS

While we're taking a pounding on trade, the competition keeps growing. Our annual trade deficit with China is already more than $200 billion. China is insinuating itself into areas that were once dominated by our own production lines. It makes parts for Boeing 757s, and the two largest American auto parts makers have factories in China. And that doesn't even begin to account for China's clear dominance in other areas, like textiles. Some economists predict that China is poised to replace the United States as the number one economic superpower within ten years. That's a scary thought.

China doesn't even *try* to play fair. The corruption is rampant. They don't think twice about stealing technology or infringing on copyrights. And anyone who has ever done business in China has encountered the blatant system of payoffs and special deals. I made several trips to China after Chrysler bought American Motors in 1987. AMC had made a deal in 1983 to build Jeeps in China, and Jeep had a factory in Beijing. The mid-level managers asked for kickbacks right up front. A guy would say, "Mr. Iacocca, I have a son who wants to go to UCLA. Who is going to pay for that?" I was surprised at how overt the pitches were. I kept replying, "Uh, we don't do things that way," but I don't think they believed me because plenty of our companies *did* play the favors game.

In recent years, as money has flowed into China, the cash grab has become more feverish. So much for the evils of capitalism! A business associate recently visited China. He told me upon his return, "So much has changed, but one thing hasn't changed—the *corruption*."

A lot of people dismiss China's competitive edge as being all about cheap labor. But there's a lot more to it than that. As *New York Times* columnist Thomas L. Friedman put it in *The*

World Is Flat, "The biggest mistake any business can make when it comes to China is thinking that it is winning only on wages and not improving quality and productivity." It's something to ponder. Wouldn't we be stunned if China started paying its workers American-style wages, and companies *still* wanted to do business there?

And we can't afford to take our eyes off India. Not too long ago, India was known for its poverty. But today India has become one of the fastest-growing economies in the world. This is in large part due to its dominance in the high technology fields. (If you think Americans are too cell-phone crazy, try walking down a city street in India. *Everyone* is plugged in all the time.)

A great key to India's emerging economy is its rapidly expanding middle class. While the American middle class struggles to stay solvent, India's has more than tripled in the last twenty years to 250 million — almost the size of the U.S. population.

LET'S ACT IN OUR OWN SELF-INTEREST, FOR A CHANGE

There's only one way to shift the trade balance. The United States has to begin to act in its own self-interest.

Some years ago, I got a lesson in the rules of self-interest from Dr. Tomito Kubo, the chairman of Mitsubishi Motors. Mitsubishi's headquarters and main factory are located in the beautiful Japanese shrine city of Kyoto. It always struck me as an odd place to put a factory. I once asked Dr. Kubo why Mitsubishi had selected such a lovely setting for its manufacturing center.

Dr. Kubo told me that the Kyoto factory had started out as Japan's major aircraft plant during World War II. It's where they built the engines for their vaunted Zero Fighter planes. Why *there*, in the midst of the shrines and gardens? Because Franklin and Eleanor Roosevelt had once visited the city while on vacation, and when the war began, President Roosevelt gave orders that Kyoto was never to be bombed.

Dr. Kubo told me, "We in Japan look out for our self-interest. What I don't understand is why your country doesn't always do the same."

Kubo was right. Self-interest is a concept we have some trouble with. It sounds so *unfriendly*. But I believe every country has an obligation to put its self-interest first. On a global scale that means devising a world trade system that strikes a balance between the two extremes of free trade and protectionism.

The way free trade operates today, it's a "win-lose" situation, and the loser is the United States. That's just nuts. There's no excuse for it. International trade is nothing more than a business deal, and every good business deal I've ever been involved in has been "win-win." The other guy comes away feeling as good as I do, or we simply don't do business together for very long. It's got to be in *my* self-interest, or I won't play; it's got to be in *his* self-interest or he won't play. The ultimate example of win-win for me was the time the financier Kirk Kerkorian called me, crowing about a deal he'd made with the developer Steve Wynn. "I bought out your friend Steve today," he said happily. "I never thought Steve would sell so low." A couple of days later, Steve

Wynn called me, bursting with satisfaction. "I never dreamed your friend Kirk would pay so much," he gloated. Each of them thought they'd really scored on the other. These two visionaries, who essentially built Las Vegas, were able to make a deal and both come away satisfied. *That*'s win-win.

WHERE'S THE LEADERSHIP ON TRADE?

The Bush administration has got to stop being so cavalier about the trade imbalance. Aren't we holding a big trump card here? Think about it. The United States is the world's shopping mall—a giant bazaar where the world sells its goods. This doesn't benefit us, and in the long run it doesn't benefit our trading partners, either. The United States can't tolerate the sky-high levels of public and private debt the trade imbalance brings. The bubble will burst, and when it does those countries that have relied almost entirely on the American market for their profits will be in serious trouble.

Sometimes I wonder, do we *deliberately* choose some of the weakest, most submissive people to be our trade negotiators? Because it's hard to understand why our trade negotiators can't talk tough. Don't they realize that the very countries with which we have the highest trade deficits are the ones that need our market the most? What would happen if Japan or China or Korea couldn't sell their products in *America*?

I once asked that question in a speech I gave to the American Chamber of Commerce in Tokyo. I said if Japan was protectionist, it was protecting the wrong market. It was protecting its market in *Japan* when it should be protecting its market in *America*.

I got a lot of publicity for that speech, and even the Japanese seemed to take me seriously for once. But *nothing* changed. Why? Because *we* didn't demand it. If I were in charge of trade policy, I'd propose that we begin to work on *freezing* the trade deficit. I'd tell the nations that have been gorging at our table for all these years that *they* have to come up with policies in their own countries to level the playing field. What do you think would happen? Well, as I said, we hold the biggest trump card of all—the American market. Don't you think it's time to play it?

X

Don't fence me in . . .
or out

Whether you're talking domestic policy or foreign policy, the context for everything we do is global. I think we've got to approach that reality with a little humility. My father used to say, "Lee, you're the head of a big, worldwide corporation. I'll bet you've met a million people. Well, that leaves billions of people you haven't met. So, keep an open mind. It's a big universe out there." My father didn't live to see the incredible explosion of global interdependence that has occurred in the past twenty years, but I think his advice would have been the same.

My friend, former astronaut Buzz Aldrin, who knows something about globalization because he's one of the few people who has seen the whole globe from the moon, sent me this piece that he said was making the rounds on the Internet. It makes the point—*vividly*:

Question: What is the truest definition of Globalization?

Answer: Princess Diana's death.

Question: How come?

Answer: An English princess with an Egyptian boyfriend crashes in a French tunnel, driving a German car with a Dutch engine, driven by a Belgian who was drunk on Scotch whiskey, followed closely by Italian Paparazzi, on Japanese motorcycles, treated by an American doctor, using Brazilian medicines. This is posted by an American, using Bill Gates' technology, and you're probably reading this on a computer that uses Taiwanese chips and a Korean monitor, assembled by Bangladeshi workers in a Singapore plant, transported by Indian lorry-drivers, hijacked by Indonesians, unloaded by Sicilian longshoremen, and trucked to you by Mexican illegals. That, my friend, is Globalization!

I'm not trying to make light of Princess Diana's death. But it kind of makes your head spin to consider how interconnected the world has become. Some people are nervous about globalization. And some people are just in denial. But it's impossible to escape it—the way the world seeps in. You can't fence the world out, and you can't fence yourself in. Technology knows no borders. As one of the first computer geeks stated, "Information wants to be free."

To fear globalization is to fear change, but like it or not, *change* is a constant in our lives.

Now I don't know about you, but every time in my life I got

secure and complacent, God threw me a curve. Looking back, I now see that it wasn't a curve, it was a challenge. A challenge I *needed*. I had to shake off my complacency and *change*. Whenever you hear anyone saying, "Let's keep doing things exactly the way we've been doing them for twenty years," watch out. A shake-up is coming.

The seasons change. Summer follows spring, and night follows day. Life is full of ups and downs. Business cycles go round and round. Events happen that rock your world: People in the family die. You get a divorce. You get fired. Your business goes under. I've been through all of these changes, and each time I've had to wake up and try something different.

Before you can deal with change, however, you have to *see* it. Then you have to *accept* it. Sometimes that's the hardest part—acknowledging and then accepting that the way you've always done business or lived your life just won't work anymore.

This is just a basic life lesson. It's true of individuals, families, and companies. And of course it's true of *nations*. There are plenty of historical examples of nations that got knocked in the head because they resisted change. In fact, you can go back and track the success and failure of any nation in the world by how open it was to change.

Imperial Spain had tons of gold and silver in the 1600s, but its empire soon collapsed because it didn't change with the times. The once-great British empire launched the industrial revolution and colonized the world. But it got dragged down by its bureaucracy and today has the lowest per capita income in Europe. The Soviet Union had more land, gold, and oil than anybody in the world. But its rigid Communist system strangled its ability to change with the times.

Japan, too, was reluctant to change. In the 1960s and early 1970s, the Japanese economy grew 10 percent a year. Some economists predicted that it would surpass the U.S. economy by the year 1998. That didn't happen. Not even close. Why? Because Japan refused to open its doors to farming, retailing, and finance. The big bust in the 1990s came because Japan had created a bubble economy—basically, an illusion of profit—and had stopped facing reality. You can't manipulate your currency decade after decade and not eventually face the consequences.

America hasn't been immune. We paid a big price for getting too comfortable after World War II. We had a conquerer's mentality, and as a result we didn't think the competition from Japan meant much. We got a little arrogant—okay, a *lot* arrogant—and we started to slide.

These days everyone is looking toward China. But for hundreds of years China was the sleeping giant. It's the oldest and most overpowering example of resistance to change.

Back in the Middle Ages, China was the preeminent nation on earth, and the most technologically advanced. Among its other contributions to civilization, it invented paper, the printing press, the compass, the telescope, and gunpowder. We in the West have benefited from the genius of China for thousands of years. But in the past, some of the really good ideas took a while to get out.

Take the wheelbarrow. The simple wheelbarrow, invented in China, took almost twelve hundred years to get to Europe. The blast furnace, used to make cast iron, took almost eighteen hundred years to get to the West. And something as simple as the common match was used in China for two thousand years before it reached the West. Since I'm of Italian heritage, the invention I'm most grateful for is noodles, which we now call pasta.

Today, you wouldn't be able to keep good ideas like these secret for very long. The world is much smaller and more open. No matter how determined you are to keep it to yourself, it's going to leak out through e-mails and phone calls and observation. It's astounding to realize, however, that until President Nixon's historic engagement with China in the early 1970s, we weren't even *talking*, let alone sharing technology. Now we know that ideas and innovation cannot be walled in or walled out.

It's instructive to consider how China became so isolated. During the fifteenth century, China suddenly turned inward due to a strong cultural conviction that its society was superior to all others. China closed its doors and refused to allow competing ideas in. Outsiders represented inferiority. Well, you know what happens when any society rests on its laurels. It grows complacent and lazy, and that's what happened in China. The powerful emperors and bureaucracy stifled innovation. The result was five centuries of stagnation.

Meanwhile, Europe came out of the Middle Ages with a completely different outlook, and began the long march toward capitalism and democracy. It began colonizing the world. America came into being because of this expansive ideology.

But today—almost overnight, it seems—we are seeing the stirring of a phenomenal cultural shift in China. It happened in large part because a daring leader stepped forward and forced China to join the twentieth century.

His name was Deng Xiaoping. For many years, Deng was in Mao Tse-tung's inner circle. But he was something of a rebel, and Mao exiled him to a tractor repair plant in a remote outpost where he was forced to become a mechanic to support himself. But he didn't complain. He worked his way back into Mao's good graces, and he went on to become one of the most influential leaders of the twentieth century.

After Mao's death in 1976, Deng took over the leadership, and he tried to bring China into the modern age. Deng saw the advantages of developing China's economy, and he tried to open up relations with the West. It was Deng who arranged a peaceful transfer of Hong Kong from British control, promising that Hong Kong would remain a capitalist nation. He introduced the idea of the "two Chinas"—one Communist, on the mainland, and one capitalist, in Hong Kong.

When I did business in China during the late eighties and early nineties, I experienced the strange schizophrenia of a nation trying to maintain Communism in a free market world. It didn't work so well. I remember on one occasion I had sold a four-cylinder engine line to a village a thousand miles north of Beijing. (By *village*, I mean an area with a population of about one million people.) Everything was controlled by the local commissar—which would be comparable to having your city council member control your business decisions. When I arrived at the commissar's office, he said, "Sorry. So sorry. I can't see you today."

I was flabbergasted. "I came all the way to China to help set up an assembly line!"

He shrugged. "My problem this morning is that I'm short of kindergarten teachers. Our business will have to wait."

Can China maintain its Communist system in a free market economy? I don't think so. Something will have to give. If you ask me, very soon there will be only *one* China, and it will be capitalist.

THE MARKET SPEAKS LOUD AND CLEAR

So let's start with this premise: First, globalization is *inescapable*. And second, because globalization is inescapable, it's *good*. That's another way of saying that what we can't prevent we must embrace.

I'm a business guy, so my instinct is to ask, How can we benefit from the growing markets of China and India? The population of China alone comprises one fifth of the world. Here in America we've tended to view that as an intimidating fact instead of a huge, lucrative market.

In the next ten years China's demand for cars will grow at a rate that is almost unthinkable. It is estimated to reach eight to ten million new cars per year. Who is going to build those cars? Today, every major car company is trying to get a foothold in China.

India is also booming. I've never heard so much moaning and groaning about anything as I've heard about India. People are burned up about outsourcing. They get annoyed when they have to go through Indian customer service representatives to get help with their American products. But from the standpoint of infusing business with creativity and opportunity, it's a great thing that India has taken this niche and run with it.

What once was a nation identified with its teeming masses and abject poverty is emerging—somewhat chaotically, but legitimately—as a partner in progress. We can welcome it, or we can shut it out. Our call.

The Las Vegas developer Steve Wynn is a good example of what it means to welcome globalization. Recently I had dinner with Steve and his wife in Las Vegas. Steve was telling me about his new resort in Macau, which is near Hong Kong. He said that since he's doing business in China, he's learning to speak mandarin Chinese. Like everything with Steve, he's totally immersing himself in the effort. He's got a full-time mandarin teacher who travels with him everywhere he goes. That's global thinking at its best.

"MR. BUSH, TEAR DOWN THAT WALL!"

The first time I visited China, in 1989, I walked along the Great Wall. It was a breathtaking experience. But what really shocked me was that about one hundred soldiers patrolling the wall were calling to me and waving copies of my autobiography, *Iacocca*. It was a touching scene until I realized they were bootlegged copies. The point is, I was seeing the old ways and the new ways all in one moment. Deng's son sent me two copies of *Iacocca* to autograph—one for himself and one for his dad. Who could have imagined it?

The biggest lesson we've learned from the Chinese, and again, from the Communists who built the Berlin Wall, is that no wall is strong enough to hold back the tide of progress or to protect its people. Now Israel is building a barrier on the West Bank. How do you think *that's* going to work out? Walls don't work.

Which brings us to the United States. Congress was happy to approve the construction of a wall along our border with Mexico to keep the illegals out—which just goes to show that Congress is always ready to respond quickly to fear. It's not so good at solving *real* problems. (For example, they forgot to *fund* the wall.)

I don't dispute that security is a legitimate concern. There's no question about that. We've been too lax for too long about devising a workable solution to the problem of illegal immigration. This is what they call a "hot button" issue. It makes politicians nervous. There's a lot of grandstanding.

But whose bright idea was it to build a three-hundred-mile wall to secure our border with Mexico? The border is two thousand miles long. That's like triple-locking the front door and leaving the back door open. But even if we built a wall that stretched the entire length of the border, it would not solve the problem.

I'll go one step further. Even if everybody agreed that a wall was a workable solution, what the hell are we doing building walls? America doesn't build walls. It tears them down. One of the most inspirational moments of the last twenty years was when Ronald Reagan stood up and said, "Mr. Gorbachev, tear down that wall." And the Berlin Wall came tumbling down.

Countries build walls when they lack the creativity to solve complex problems. And there is nothing more complex than figuring out how we're going to relate to the world outside our borders. While we're at it, we have to have a plan for dealing with the eleven million illegal immigrants that are already here.

My immigrant father taught me that there is only one reason why people leave the country of their birth to go somewhere else: *jobs*. Every immigrant, legal or illegal, comes to America because he wants to improve his lot in life. Most immigrants work hard and make great sacrifices to create better futures for their children. It's the American dream.

I've often wondered where the United States would be today if we hadn't opened our arms so wide during the great immigration wave of the last century. The seventeen million people, like my parents, who passed through Ellis Island gave birth to one hundred million offspring, and those offspring have made this country what it is today.

In 1982, when President Reagan asked me to serve as chairman of the Statue of Liberty–Ellis Island Centennial Commission, how could I refuse? I had plenty on my plate running Chrysler, but I knew I had to accept as a tribute to my parents— in memory of my father, who'd died in 1973, and for my mother, who was still alive. And we accomplished a miracle that would have made my father proud. We raised half a billion dollars and by July, 4, 1986, the Statue of Liberty was ready for unveiling.

Liberty Weekend dawned with the Great Lady standing tall in New York Harbor, and Ellis Island on its way to being fully restored. In ceremonies that weekend many inspirational words were spoken. I can still remember my feelings of pride and hope. I think we need to be reminded every once in a while of who we are, and what kind of nation we've promised to be. Not a nation that builds walls, but a nation that lifts a lamp to light the way.

EMBRACING THE GLOBE

Today, more than twenty years later, we have a rare opportunity to once again demonstrate our commitment to being a global leader. But the challenges have changed. Now leadership involves not just lending a hand, but also lending an ear—respecting the cultures and insights of other nations. There is a lot of enthusiasm for the *idea* of globalization, but the *reality* was that people tended to stay in their own corners.

You can lead nations to the global marketplace, but you can't make them *think* globally or *behave* globally. And if this age of globalization is going to be a force for good on the planet, that has to happen.

Around the time the Statue of Liberty and Ellis Island were being refurbished, I began to think about what I could do to improve the spirit of global understanding and cooperation.

The idea for the Iacocca Institute at Lehigh University emerged from the question, How do you go about building global leadership? How do you demonstrate to people from different worlds that their commonalities are greater than their differences?

Thanks to the receptivity of my alma mater, Lehigh University, a course was established to teach students how to be competitive in the global marketplace. Then, about eleven years ago, a guy named Dick Brandt came along with a vision for a global leadership school, called the Global Village for Future Leaders of Business and Industry. Dick sold me and Lehigh University on the idea of globalizing the world one young mind at a time.

Dick's concept was to create a summer training course for promising young businesspeople and entrepreneurs from around the world. We ran a pilot program in the summer of 1996 with representatives from twenty-five countries. There were a lot of kinks to iron out, but I was sold. This was an investment worth making.

Dick's an interesting guy. Before he took on the program he was a vice president at AT&T, running its international division. In his work Dick became increasingly convinced that the biggest barrier to cooperation, whether in business or government, was that we didn't understand each other. Dick always says, "We're doing our piece for world peace," and I think that's true. But the funny thing is, there isn't much talk about war and peace in the Global Village. The spirit of understanding seems to happen automatically through immersion. It's awfully hard to dismiss someone who's living, eating, and working side by side with you in an intense setting.

The diversity of the students is impressive. If you visit the Global Village you might find an engineer from Singapore, a Pakistani fashion designer, a Peruvian banker, a shipper from Ghana, a farmer from Mexico, a lawyer from Slovenia, and a doctor from Italy. They all want to succeed.

In the early years of the Global Village, we learned our cultural lessons right along with the students. Here's an example. In the beginning we provided students with three meals a day of old-fashioned Pennsylvania Dutch cooking. But we started to see that the students were getting fat. Most of these kids weren't used to eating so much food—especially all the meat and potatoes. We were a little embarrassed about it. Dick realized that food was a core concept. How you eat, where you eat, and what you eat has a lot to do with your identity. Dick thought if we could provide a place for students to cook their own meals, we could solve the problem, plus cut the price of tuition by a thousand dollars. We took over a sorority house at Lehigh and set up a kitchen where students could prepare foods from their own lands. The cooking experiment became so successful that Dick incorporated it into the curriculum. Certain nights were set aside for students to showcase their ethnic cooking for the entire group—often served in traditional garb. It became a highlight of the course.

The most powerful part of the Global Village program is the business project. We put teams together and send them out to cooperating businesses in the Lehigh Valley, with the task of solving a *real* business problem. In these cross-cultural teams, the students are under pressure to perform by working through their cultural differences. As Dick tells them, "Your competitive edge in a global society will be your ability to transcend differences and collaborate."

The graduation ceremony at the Global Village is an elaborate black-tie dinner dance. Every time I attend the event, I'm blown away. Last year, the 2006 graduating class consisted of eighty-seven students, and many of them arrived at the dinner wearing beautiful traditional garb. It was a bittersweet moment for them, because they would soon be returning to their countries and saying goodbye to some of the best friends they'd ever made. It was touching to watch them interact. Some of them had been taught their whole lives to hate the very people they were now embracing.

I saw a young guy ask an Arab girl who was wearing a veil to dance, and I thought, "Wow! This is globalization." I saw two students, one from Beirut and one from Tel Aviv, hugging each other and crying. When they'd left their homes for Pennsylvania, there had been no fighting between their countries. Now there were bombings every day. They didn't know what they would face when they returned home, but they knew one thing: *They* were not enemies. This is America's greatest advantage. People can come here from all over the world and live together in peace.

I said a few words at the dinner. I told the graduates I was writing a book about leadership, and I asked them to help me out. "Write to me," I said, "and tell me what globalization means to you. Is it a good thing? Who are the global leaders today?"

They took me seriously. Their responses came from all corners of the world, filled with optimism and passion. *Yes* to globalization. *Yes* to cooperation. Their enthusiasm was infectious, and I like to think it will *infect* the world.

PART THREE

IS CAPITALISM
LETTING US DOWN?

XI

Where does all the money go?

Dick Brandt shared an interesting insight about the Global Village students recently. He said, "The international kids are struck by how much we *have* here in America, how much time we spend watching TV commercials, and *especially* how much time we spend shopping and spending. They don't *get* the concept of shopping as *entertainment*. For them shopping is what you do when you *need* something."

Dick added that he doesn't see much *envy* of American consumerism. I guess the kids are smart enough to know that having a lot of *stuff* is not a measure of real success. We preach the capitalist way like it's a religion, but you have to wonder if it's letting us down. When advertising slogans are better known than the Ten Commandments or the Bill of Rights, when shopping malls are our places of worship, when bad behavior is justified as long as it leads to profit, when debt is justified as long as it leads to a plasma TV, and when the measure of a person is the kind of car he drives, maybe it's time to ask whether we've corrupted the very notion of capitalism.

Believe it or not, capitalism originated as a system for the little guy. It replaced feudalism, in which a few wealthy owners had all the power and money and the common person had nothing. It was a noble ideal.

The great economist Milton Friedman, who died in 2006 at the age of ninety-four, once said, "The problem of social organization is how to set up an arrangement under which greed will do the least harm. Capitalism is that kind of a system." Friedman believed that you couldn't have freedom without capitalism. The problem is that any system, even a good one, can get rusty over time if we're not vigilant. And we've become pretty lazy about our system. Money has stopped *meaning* anything to us.

When I was growing up in the 1940s, a million seemed like infinity. All those zeroes! If someone was a millionaire, that meant they had more money than *God*. I never heard anyone say, "You're one in a *billion*." A million was plenty good enough.

I was just getting the hang of a billion, when people started talking about a *trillion*. Today our country casually spends a trillion dollars the way we once spent a billion. Where does it end? What's the next level? I guess it's *quadrillion*. Then *zillion*? I'm not sure. Let's just say it's a *lot*.

WHERE DOES ALL THE MONEY COME FROM?

So where does the government get all this money to spend? The short answer is we *borrow* it.

If you have a credit card, you can understand what's happening with our government today. It's the same thing. Not that you're running up the big numbers—even if you have teenagers. But the concept is no different. When you borrow money on a credit card, and you don't pay it back within thirty days, there's a penalty called "interest." And if you keep borrowing, your debt grows and so does your interest. When you get your credit card bill, the minimum payment only covers the interest. It doesn't touch the principal. The more debt you have, the harder it is to pay *anything* off on the principal. (The average American household has twelve credit cards, so if you're like most Americans, you're probably feeling the pinch.)

Now, apply that same idea to government spending. If we spend *less* in a year than we collect, we have a surplus. If we spend *more* than we collect, we have a deficit. That's when we get out the credit cards and start borrowing.

Where do we go to borrow money? To other countries. Almost 50 percent of U.S. debt is held by foreign banks. We go to China, Japan, Saudi Arabia, or one of our other lenders, and we say, "Listen, we need $300 billion to pay for the war in Iraq. That'll get us started. And we need $600 billion for a permanent tax cut. Our kids will pay you back."

Our national debt is a record $8.5 trillion. The interest on that alone is $406 billion. We can scrape together enough money to pay the interest, but we're not even touching the principal. That means the money we shell out in taxes doesn't buy one new cop or one new schoolteacher. It just pays the interest on what we already owe. When we actually want to *do* something, we borrow more.

You know what a drag it is when you're in so much debt that you're just paying interest on your credit cards. All that money and nothing to show for it. Not a new sofa or a winter coat or a vacation. It's the same with our government. When we make our $406 billion annual interest payment, we get a big fat nothing for it.

Shouldn't we be just a little bit pissed off? You'd think if we were going to go into debt on such a grand scale, we'd at least have something to show for it. Like better health care. Or roads that aren't falling apart. Or cheaper gas. But the government seems to have run up our credit cards without buying anything we can use.

In 1989, when the national debt was considered a real crisis, the big National Debt Clock went up in Times Square. This was during Bush senior's administration when a national debt of $2.7 trillion actually shocked the nation. There were pictures of people standing on the sidewalk gaping up at the clock as the numbers raced up. It was pretty mesmerizing—especially since it also included the share every family in America owed. Then one day, when the total had reached $5 trillion, the National Debt Clock disappeared. Well, today it's back, and now the numbers are racing up toward $9 trillion. But the crowds aren't gathering. Nobody's gaping. We're used to it. We've lost our ability to be shocked.

But we'd better open our eyes. Like that old curmudgeon Senator Everett Dirksen used to say, "A billion here, a billion there, and pretty soon you're talking about real money."

That's the thing you have to remember. The money is *real*. How popular do you think Bush's tax cuts would be if people understood we're borrowing from *China* to pay for them? Is that fiscal responsibility? It wouldn't pass muster in most households.

Wouldn't you like to see our government show a little budgeting discipline—just like you have to do at home? Maybe if the citizens got a statement every year, they'd demand it. Based on the current national debt, your statement would read something like this:

> *Dear Mr. and Mrs. America,*
>   *Your family's share of the national debt is currently $115,000. Would you like that amount deferred to your grandchildren?*

Too bad we didn't listen to Thomas Jefferson. He said, "To preserve our independence, we must not let our rulers load us with perpetual debt."

SPENDING GONE WILD

When you think of it, isn't the President really just the CEO of America? Under George Bush's leadership, we've spent half a trillion (and counting) on Iraq, and the people there don't even have dependable electricity yet. Then we topped off our spending spree with the huge tax cut, which mostly went to the wealthiest Americans. They like to say that the tax-cut windfall is going to "trickle down" to average Americans. I'll tell you what's trickling down: the *debt*. Because for every dollar our government doesn't take in from taxes, that's one less dollar going to pay off the debt, and the interest keeps building. This trickle-down business is more like water torture.

It bears mentioning that Bill Clinton, one of those so-called tax-and-spend liberals, had a $559 billion surplus his last four years in office. I've coined a new phrase for the current administration: *tax-cut-and-spend conservatives.*

Now, I've heard Dick Cheney say repeatedly, "Reagan proved deficits don't matter," and I just have to shake my head. What is he talking about? Maybe he means they don't matter to *him*, since he's worth between $30 and $100 million. But I think most Americans would feel pretty nervous about having half the country's debt owned by foreigners. Twenty-five years ago we were the largest creditor nation in the world. Now we're the largest *debtor* nation.

We are in danger of becoming a colony—of not owning our own country. How did that happen to the richest nation in the world?

A SIMPLE BUSINESS LESSON

In business, the budget-cutting process is pretty simple. You get your key people in a room and you say, "Sales are down, and costs are up. We've got to cut ten percent out of the budget. Come back tomorrow and tell me what you're going to give up." And everyone looks miserable, but no one says, "Boss, we can't do it. We need to spend ten percent more than we're taking in."

In business, people get it. If a company spends more than it earns, it goes belly-up. In government, it's all smoke and mirrors. It's Alice in Wonderland down the rabbit hole.

I'll tell you one thing. Any businessperson who has to meet a payroll every week learns the value of money pretty fast. I'll never forget how I learned that lesson the hard way at Chrysler. It was shortly after I'd joined the company, and I was beginning to get a terrible feeling in my gut that we were in big trouble. One Friday morning I asked my CFO, Jerry Greenwald, how much real *cash* he could lay on my desk by five o'clock that afternoon. He said, "About a million, give or take."

Only a *million*? Then I asked him, "What's our payroll every Friday?" He said, "About two hundred million, give or take."

That's when I knew we were bankrupt. When you're responsible for meeting a weekly payroll, money gets *real* pretty fast. Unfortunately, the government seems to have lost all sight of this. I learned that, too, when I tried to pay back Chrysler's government loan.

I went to the White House to deliver the $1.2 billion check to President Reagan. In the Oval Office, I explained to the President that the check was a fake. "No one has ever paid back the government before," I explained. "They said it would take about thirty days to figure out who it should be written out to."

President Reagan laughed hysterically, slapping his knee. "You've got to be kidding me," he said. "That's what's wrong with the federal government." In other words, there were no IN baskets, only OUT baskets. With Reagan still laughing, I put a hold on the check, and kept the $10 million of interest it generated in a month.

WE'RE PIGGING OUT

It's hard for our government to exercise responsibility in spending when the citizenry has such a bad case of the *gimmies*. You don't see that many political campaigns built around paying down the national debt. It's not very sexy. It's a simple fact that the people who get elected are the ones who give out the goodies, not the ones who take them away. Look what happened to Jimmy Carter when he told Americans to turn off their lights and start wearing sweaters. Look what happened to the first President Bush when he had to go back on his promise not to raise taxes. Nobody runs for office on the slogan "Read my lips: I'll raise your taxes."

You're more likely to hear "Vote for me, and I'll find some money for your pet project."

It's called pork. Billions are spent every year for individual pork-barrel projects that get people elected. A Hall of Fame here, a bridge to nowhere there. It adds up.

I can't really blame Americans for not taking the national debt seriously. Why should they? It seems like every time the government wants to spend money on a pet project or a tax cut or a war, they find it.

I propose that we take back control of our money. How? By

voting for people who will honor their commitment to the citizens of this country. It's our right. It's also our obligation. Why don't we start by NOT voting for the candidate who promises tax cuts. Why don't we start by demanding a *National Borrowing Freeze*. Let's cut up the credit cards.

As I mentioned earlier, when I was chairman of the Statue of Liberty–Ellis Island Centennial Commission, we raised millions of dollars from ordinary people all over America. We got almost $2 million from schoolchildren sending in their nickels and dimes. One morning I opened a letter with two one-dollar bills attached. The letter was written in a child's hand. "Dear Mr. Iacocca," it read. "Here's my allowance for the week. Spend it wisely." That got me. *Spend it wisely.* The future generations are depending on us to use our heads. Are we up to the task?

XII

Will we ever trust corporate America again?

A lot of corporate executives must have been paying close attention in 1987 when the actor Michael Douglas uttered those famous words in the movie *Wall Street*: "Greed is good." They took it to heart.

When I was a kid, the nuns hammered us with the Seven Deadly Sins. Those were the sins that doomed your immortal soul. Serious stuff. Greed was on top of the list. I didn't really understand what they were getting at with the word *deadly*, but I figured it out pretty quick when I got into business.

Greed has always been with us, especially in the money-changing professions. But has it ever been this bad? I don't think so. The most prevalent motto of corporate America seems to be greed. You ask someone to name a top business leader, and they think of the guy they just saw being led away in handcuffs.

Greed is big, but I'm not letting *envy* off the hook. That's a deadly sin, too. Sometimes I think the real culprit is envy. A

CEO looks at another CEO, and says, "Hey, he's making fifty million, and I'm only making thirty million. I'm in the same industry, and I'm better than he is. I should be making *sixty* million." That's how the executive compensations spiral up. Nobody says, "Well, thirty million is pretty good." So envy can trump greed.

When I was young, I'd look at the CEOs of the big companies, and I'd say, "Wow! That's where I want to be someday. They're the cream of the crop." In those days, CEOs were the most admired people in the country, and car salesmen were the least admired. Today, car salesmen rate above CEOs on the admiration scale. What's going on? Is it a few bad apples, or is the whole barrel decayed?

A HECKUVA JOB, KENNY BOY

My mother always taught me not to speak ill of the dead, but I have to say a few words about Kenneth Lay, may he rest in peace.

I know that some people found it hard to think of Ken Lay as a bad guy. He had such an *engaging* manner, such a fresh, all-American face. He was charming. He loved his wife. He didn't fit the image of a robber baron. He was the CEO of Enron, an energy company based in Houston—the poster boy of American success.

And how many villains have cute nicknames given to them by the President of the United States? "Kenny Boy" just didn't seem like the kind of guy who would cook the books and drive his company into the ground. And he didn't seem like the kind of guy who would defraud his workers. But that's what he did. When it became obvious to him that Enron was going under, Lay did two things. First, he unloaded his own stock, making $70 million on the spot. Then he froze his workers' stock, which was invested in their pension plans, so they couldn't withdraw the money. When the collapse finally happened, Enron's stock was worth thirty-five cents a share. Most of the employees lost their pensions, along with their jobs.

We're not talking about small change here. There were employees with over thirty years at the company whose pension plans had swelled to between $500,000 and a million—and they were left with nothing. Others had saved $100,000 or $200,000, and they were looking forward to retiring with twice that amount. In all, the Enron collapse resulted in employee pension losses of almost $1 billion.

In 2006, Ken Lay was convicted on six counts of fraud and conspiracy, and was awaiting sentencing when he suddenly dropped dead of a massive heart attack. I guess in Kenny Boy's case, greed really *was* a deadly sin. There's a bright side, though—at least, for Kenny Boy's wife. Because he conveniently died before sentencing, Lay's conviction was thrown out. That means not a penny of his fortune will go to the pension-poor employees he robbed. I guess those former Enron employees will have to get their rewards in heaven.

PAY FOR PERFORMANCE—A NOVEL IDEA

Guys like Ken Lay finally got people paying attention to how outlandish executive compensation was getting. But the thing

that most people, including me, find unbelievable is how many
executives get huge pay packages even though they're doing *terrible* jobs of running their companies.

What kind of capitalist system is that? Whatever happened
to "pay for performance"?

Okay—time for full disclosure. I made a lot of money as
CEO of Chrysler. Some people probably thought I made *too
much* money. But the reason I made money was because most
of my income was directly tied to the stock price. And the stock
price went up 800 percent because we were doing so well. Get
it? *Pay for performance.* It's the only way.

Unfortunately, times seem to have changed. Now it's no
longer a requirement that a CEO make a company profitable in
order to earn big bucks.

A few years ago, it got so bad that *Fortune* magazine published a cover featuring a smiling pig in a business suit, with the
headline "Have They No Shame?" That was the year the
highest-paid CEOs in the country were heading the worst-performing companies. How do you explain that?

You always hear, "We've got to pay big bucks if we want to
attract the top talent." Huh? Is this a new definition of talent—
the ability to *lose* money?

The guys taking these monstrous salaries and pensions
are thumbing their noses at the shareholders. It's got to stop. So,
how do we stop it? Well, the problem starts with the good old
boys (and girls) on the boards of directors.

INCEST IN THE BOARDROOM

Incest isn't one of the Seven Deadly Sins, but maybe it should be. Today's corporate boards are extremely incestuous: Insiders bring in other insiders who bring in other insiders. Most boards serve at the pleasure of the CEO. It's not supposed to be that way, but that's the reality. I've been there and experienced it myself. If a CEO is powerful, he makes a board his own. Although the board's job is to represent the shareholders, its members are chosen by a hired hand.

The job of a corporate board of directors is to keep chief executives on the straight and narrow, to review their plans and priorities, and to hold them accountable. But it can be very comfortable and clubby. When I first got to Chrysler, we had a crisis board, so everyone worked very hard. There were some terrific business minds on that board, including the guy who hired me, Bill Hewlett of Hewlett Packard. Later, when I got to select my own board, I looked for people with the best reputations, and they recommended others. I thought I assembled a strong board. But there's no question it was an inner circle.

There are some nice perks that usually go with being a director. In exchange for eight to ten days a year, directors earn compensations that can range from $50,000 to $100,000. Some get pensions, stock awards, free medical and dental care, and the use of private corporate aircraft. If you're on the board of a car company you get a new car delivered to you a couple of times a year.

I'm not saying there aren't a lot of conscientious board members in corporate America. Probably the majority are conscientious. What's missing is *leadership*. Leaders don't just take things at face value. They ask hard questions. They hold CEOs accountable.

The members of corporate boards are not secret, but unless you're a media hound like Ross Perot was when he was on the General Motors board, most directors try to keep their names out of the news. And when something goes really wrong—like Enron—everyone runs for the showers. They don't want to be tainted. Unfortunately, there's no real accountability for boards.

The most infamous board right now is the one that governs the New York Stock Exchange. Although it's a nonprofit entity, the board approved a pay package for its former CEO, Richard Grasso, that included $140 million in deferred compensation. The compensation committee of the board was handpicked by Grasso himself, and it was mostly comprised of representatives from NYSE-listed companies over which Grasso had regulatory control. Now *that's* a fox in the henhouse! New York Governor Elliott Spitzer thought so, too. When he was attorney general, Spitzer sued Grasso to get some of the money back. Grasso was forced to step down, but to this day he claims to be outraged by the suggestion that he's not worth the money. (If you're keeping track, that's the deadly sin of pride. Also wrath.)

Another recent eyebrow-raiser was the golden retirement package awarded to Lee Raymond, former CEO and chairman of ExxonMobil. Raymond received more than $400 million in total compensation. You tell that to the folks who are pumping three- and four-dollar-a-gallon gas and you might have a riot on your hands. They're already pissed off that Exxon-Mobil is showing record profits on their backs.

ExxonMobil employees have a legitimate gripe, too. In spite of those record profits, the company has underfunded its pension plan by $11.2 billion—the most of any company on record. How do they explain that? Were they afraid they'd have to shave a few bucks off Raymond's package if they funded the pension plan? What's especially galling is that U.S. taxpayers are on the hook for defaulted pension plans.

Where is the accountability to the workers who spend their lives building equity, with the promise that they'll be taken care of when they retire? How can you say to them, "Sorry, our contract with you is no longer valid?" The scandalous robbery of middle-class pensions must be investigated. It's almost as if the rule has become golden parachutes for execs and a kick in the teeth for workers.

WINDFALLS OF WAR

If there were a Hall of Shame for corporate greed, you'd have to include Halliburton, the world's largest oil and gas services company, with subsidiaries in a variety of industries. The war in Iraq has been a windfall for Halliburton. Maybe I'm getting cynical in my old age, but I wonder if it has anything to do with Vice President Dick Cheney. Before he appointed himself Vice President of the United States, Cheney was CEO of Halliburton. Strangely, Cheney's official White House biography, which is published on the Web, doesn't mention his job at Halliburton. I guess he forgot.

Halliburton and its subsidiaries just happen to be the chief beneficiaries of the rebuilding efforts in Iraq. So far, they've been awarded no-bid contracts of about $11 billion. If a job needs to be done, Halliburton's your company. It has mastered the art of the no-bid contract.

There have been numerous scandals about the way Halliburton has spent our money. The U.S. Army reports that Halliburton has overcharged the government about $128 million for fuel transportation and food services. The Halliburton subsidiary KBR, which is the main contractor responsible for restoring Iraq's oil industry, has made little progress. There are accusations of kickbacks and other outright frauds. And of course the gigantic Super Bowl party the company threw its workers in Baghdad, with big-screen TVs and tubs of chicken wings and tacos. All billed to the American taxpayer.

In spite of Halliburton's many irregularities in Iraq, after Hurricane Katrina hit the Gulf Coast, one of its subsidiaries was awarded a $29.8 million, no-bid contract for cleanup work. I hope the citizens of the Gulf Coast are enjoying their trailers!

Cheney insists that it's purely coincidental that Halliburton is the beneficiary of so much government largesse. He has said repeatedly, "I have absolutely no influence, involvement, or knowledge of federal government contracts." It's a strange thing to say, because I think that's part of his job description.

When Cheney became Vice President, he was required to sever all ties with his former company, which he did—sort of. He still retains unexercised stock options and deferred salary. His stock options alone have risen more than three thousand percent since 2004—from a value of about $250,000 to more than $8 million. I don't think that's what they mean by *severing* ties. It all amounts to an extremely generous retirement package.

Now, Cheney might be one of those rare guys who walks the straight and narrow and does the right thing, regardless of whether he benefits personally. But even if this is so, shouldn't he try to avoid the *appearance* of a conflict of interest? If you look at the raw facts, you might conclude that our Vice President is moonlighting as CEO of Halliburton.

TRY A LITTLE VIRTUE

So, those are some of the biggest sinners in the world of corporate greed. For the solution, I have to go back to basics. In fact, the answer is so simple it's a wonder I even have to spell it out: Instead of living by the deadly sins, corporate America should try living by some of the virtues.

> Instead of greed, how about generosity.
> Instead of envy, try a little charity.
> Instead of pride, show some humility.
> Instead of wrath, let's see composure.

Our capitalist system holds the promise that every American can succeed, but if we don't infuse it with some humane values, it deteriorates into a winner-take-all setup, which doesn't really serve our free enterprise system *or* our common good.

Let me tell you a story about a company that prospered under the worst circumstances because it took care of its employees. This one involves leadership in a crisis.

Before September 11, 2001, James Dunne III, one of

three managing partners of the small investing firm of Sandler O'Neill & Partners, wasn't that interested in the business. In fact, that morning he wasn't at his office at the World Trade Center. He was on a golf course trying to qualify for an amateur tournament. Being a goof-off saved his life. The other two partners, along with sixty-four employees, died in the terrorist attacks.

It looked like the firm was going to go out of business. Nobody believed that Dunne was capable of resurrecting it. But Dunne turned out to be one of those leaders who is born in a crisis. Not only did he bring the firm back, he made it larger, stronger, and better.

When I read about this guy, I was impressed by two things: one was his passion, and the other was his commitment to the people who worked in his company—including those who were lost on 9/11. The first thing Dunne did, before the smoke had even cleared, was tell the families of the victims that the firm was going to take care of them, somehow, some way. In 2001, he paid out salaries, bonuses, and the proceeds of trades as if the employees were still coming to work every day. He arranged full pensions, and set up a foundation to pay for the educations of all the children who'd lost their parents. He arranged for psychological counseling for everyone in the firm.

When clients heard of the firm's generosity, they flocked to it. When competitors found out, they lent a hand. Workers felt energized and motivated. The firm was more successful than ever.

I have to say, it makes me feel good to read stories like that, and I'll bet it has the same effect on most people. When true leadership is being practiced, it never fails to make the heart soar. And, of course, we always like to see the good guys win.

And while we're on the subject of sin and virtue, I'd like to say a word about redemption. You can be down so low that you think your life is over. But redemption is always possible if you choose it. Look at Mike Milken. In the 1980s, Milken was flying high as the "Junk Bond King." To a lot of people he personified the rampant greed of Wall Street. Then he fell hard when he was charged with ninety-eight counts of racketeering and fraud. Milken seemed like a ruined man. He served almost two years in prison and ended up paying $1 billion in fines and settlements. And to top it off, the same month he was released from prison, Mike was diagnosed with advanced prostate cancer. That was thirteen years ago. Today, Mike Milken personifies charity, not greed. His foundation has given hundreds of millions of dollars to medical research and education. We're good friends and we share a commitment to finding medical cures. Mike's too busy to worry about whether his legacy will be as a sinner or a saint. But in my book he's been redeemed.

DOING WELL BY DOING GOOD

Let me share another story about a company that I've been privileged to be a part of. It's an example of a new kind of business philosophy called common-good capitalism. I think of it as the dragon slayer of corporate greed.

NuSkin is a Utah company that produces natural skin care products. When it was established in 1984, its Mormon founders wanted to do more than just make money. Mormons are do-gooders by nature. They actually believe that companies have an obligation to contribute to the social welfare.

In 1996, NuSkin established the Force for Good Foundation, an arm of the company that supports relief efforts and community development projects all over the world. Twenty-five cents of every dollar made by selling NuSkin products goes straight into the foundation. And *this* is impressive: *100 percent* of the foundation's money goes to its projects. NuSkin covers all of the foundation's overhead and operating costs.

In 2002 I was approached by Blake Roney, the chairman and founder of NuSkin, and Truman Hunt, the president. They told me about a new foundation they were starting called Nourish the Children. They knew from the work my foundation had done on finding a cure for diabetes that I was interested in nutrition. And they guessed—correctly—that I would appreciate their brand of common-good capitalism. As a businessman, I was impressed by the quality of NuSkin's products and its large worldwide distribution force. This was a *well-run* company. But what really got me hooked was NuSkin's plan to end world hunger. I signed on, and I've been chairman of Nourish the Children's advisory board ever since.

Here's the way it works. Pharmanex, a division of NuSkin that makes nutritional supplements, teamed up with some leading experts on malnutrition to find out what nutrient mix can bring a child back from starvation. They then created a nutrient-dense meal packet, called VitaMeal, that would meet all the needs of a malnourished child.

Nourish the Children uses reputable relief agencies to distribute VitaMeal to needy children all over the world, including right here in the United States. So far, about seventy million meals have been distributed. The funding is mostly through NuSkin—a combination of company product donations and voluntary product donations from the global distributors and their customers. NuSkin encourages its employees to become Ambassadors—that is, to donate at least four bags of VitaMeal every month, and to enlist others to do so, too. And they reward employees who become Ambassadors. It's kind of hard to get your head around the idea that a corporation would tell its workers that feeding hungry children is good for their corporate career paths.

Blake Roney once told me, "Nourish the Children is five percent of what we *do*, but it's ninety-five percent of who we *are*." Whenever I pick up my newspaper and read another story about corporate greed, I think about Nourish the Children. I'll bet most people have never heard of it. Wouldn't it be great if we read more business stories that gave us an inspiring lift and fewer stories that made us sick to our stomachs? And wouldn't it be a wonderful thing if corporate America got the idea that the best way to do well is by doing good?

XIII

Chrysler's lesson: Resist the urge to merge

In life we all have high points and low points. Sometimes you're up and the sky's the limit. Other times you're down and you're sweating bullets. The bad times lead to negative thoughts and you wonder, how the hell did I get into this mess?

When I look back over almost fifty years in the car business, I see some real *doozies* on both the up and down sides of the scale. Introducing the Mustang in 1964 at the New York World's Fair was a magic moment in my life. I was on a high then, and the Mustang's success propelled me into the presidency of Ford in 1970. Me, an immigrant kid from Allentown, Pennsylvania, named president of the second-largest company in the world. Who would have dreamed it?

Well, with the good comes the bad, and if being president of Ford was a high, being fired in 1978 from the same job was the pits. One day I was in the catbird seat and the next day I was reading the want ads. I got another job all right, but it was more like going from the frying pan into the fire. Chrysler was on the verge of bankruptcy. But with a lot of sacrifice, hard work, and luck, we turned the company around.

When I retired from Chrysler at the end of 1992, I felt pretty satisfied with what I'd achieved. Chrysler was on top of the world. It was the perfect time to take a bow and exit. In the years after my retirement, things just got better. Chrysler was making a lot of money—something like a billion dollars every quarter. The minivan was a cash cow, the Jeep Grand Cherokee and Dodge Ram pickup were selling like crazy, we had 4,000 profitable dealers, a brand-new $1.5 billion research center, and $12 billion in cash. Chrysler was the lowest cost producer and the most profitable car company in the world, with sales of two and a half million cars and light trucks a year. It was a huge success story.

So on the morning of January 12, 1998, when I woke up to the news that Chrysler had just been sold to the Germans, it knocked me for a loop. Of all the highs and lows I'd experienced, this was the lowest low. The news hit me where it hurt—deep in the groin. I was sick, I couldn't sleep, I had a bad case of agita. How could this happen? I kept playing it over in my mind. I gave fifteen years of my life to saving that company and now I wondered if it was worth it. How could they take Walter Chrysler's venerable company, a great American institution, and name it after a *German*?

Was I emotional about the surprise announcement? You're damn right I was emotional. The merger didn't make sense at all. Chrysler was doing great. It should have been calling the shots on its own terms. It held all the cards. How did the company get maneuvered into giving it all away? I'm not kidding when I tell you that day was rock bottom for me. A real *lower-than-whale-shit* moment.

What happened to DaimlerChrysler is a cautionary tale for every business that might be contemplating a merger. Don't make any moves until you read this chapter.

THE WORST DECISION I EVER MADE

I'll always believe that if I hadn't chosen Bob Eaton to succeed me as chief executive at Chrysler, it would still be a strong, profitable, *American* car company. Eaton came to Chrysler from GM, and he got high marks on paper. But he just didn't get it. Never did. That was *my* mistake. I can't even blame the board. They trusted me. Eaton was my call, and I screwed up.

Then, a couple of years after I retired, I inadvertently helped trigger a panic in Eaton that led to the whole sorry mess. In 1995, the billionaire financier Kirk Kerkorian, who owned 10 percent of Chrysler stock, came to me with an interesting idea. He wanted to buy Chrysler and take it private. He thought the stock was greatly undervalued. Kerkorian convinced me that taking Chrysler private was a win-win deal for everyone involved. We'd offer Chrysler shareholders $55 a share—a 40 percent premium over the market price of $39. Five percent of the company would be given to the management. And, most important, 20 percent of the company would be given to the workers.

I believed that this would not be a hostile takeover, that Eaton was on board, and that the cash was in hand. But this proved not to be true. The deal never got off the ground. What it did do was trigger a panic in Eaton. He became obsessed with warding off any future takeover bids.

This was a critical moment for Chrysler, when cooler heads might have prevailed. Eaton should have used it as an opportunity to evaluate the company's future. He was sitting on top of the lowest-cost producer in the world, and he was running scared? Try explaining that one. Instead of thinking it through, Eaton plunged headlong into the merger with Daimler-Benz.

Eaton believed Chrysler had to have a European partner to survive. He got outmaneuvered by the slick Daimler-Benz CEO, Jürgen E. Schrempp. What was Schrempp bringing to the table? Mercedes had only 1 percent of the American market, and no one could explain what the two companies had in common. I said at the time that it was the culture clash heard round the world—and I was right.

When the deal was announced, Schrempp hailed it as "a merger of equals." That was a joke. You didn't have to be a business wizard to see that it was a takeover. Schrempp was only interested in preserving Daimler's heritage and the Karl Benz legacy. What about Walter P. Chrysler's legacy—or *mine*? Who was defending *them*? If there was going to be a merger, shouldn't the surviving company have been the great American car company?

Instead, the new company was incorporated in Germany, which meant it couldn't even be listed on the S&P 500 Index. Daimler held 57 percent of the stock, while Chrysler held only 43 percent. The decision makers were in Stuttgart and the bankers were in Berlin. The pretense that there would be co-

CEOs—Schrempp in Stuttgart and Eaton in Auburn Hills—was completely unworkable. For one thing, whether you're running a company or you're running a country, the buck has to stop *somewhere*. You wouldn't have two presidents, two kings, two popes. It'd never work. There never really *were* co-CEOs at DaimlerChrysler, because the same day the deal was announced, Eaton told the world he'd be retiring in three years and Schrempp would become the sole CEO. So, who were they kidding with all the talk about co-CEOs? What you had was one CEO (Schrempp) and one lame duck (Eaton).

Then there was the question of the new entity's name. What's in a name? *Everything.*Originally, Eaton had proposed that the company be named ChryslerDaimler-Benz. Schrempp told him that was a deal breaker. It had to be DaimlerChrysler or the merger was off. Eaton wanted the deal so badly that he didn't even try to call Schrempp's bluff. Instead, he told the board that the name didn't matter. He told them it was merely cosmetic. Yeah, tell that to Walter P. Chrysler, who must have been turning over in his grave. Eaton acknowledged that the name might have a temporary negative effect on worker morale, but they'd get over it. And not a single person on the Chrysler board stood up and said, "No. We will not betray our American roots."

I'd like to see the minutes of the board meeting when this merger was presented. Was everyone asleep? Did they think they were just innocent bystanders? I can tell you they weren't asking any hard questions. Maybe they were too dazzled by the idea of a short-term bump in the stock price. I doubt that anybody asked, "Where is the synergy between these two companies?"

It became immediately apparent that there *was* no synergy in the cultures of the two companies. Mercedes was stiff and formal, with layers upon layers of committees and subcommittees. Chrysler was loose and creative, something of a renegade in corporate culture. Its divisions were lean and market-driven. Mercedes came in with stacks of black books and a cast of thousands.

Cultural synergy is important, but the real nuts and bolts of a successful merger is in product-and-sales synergy. From the product standpoint, the goal is to spread the costs over more units, by sharing product programs and platforms. The more common parts you can use under the skin of the vehicles, the more cost-effective you'll be. In fact, the opportunity for product synergy, leading to huge savings, was one of the primary goals of the merger. It was announced that DaimlerChrysler expected to save $1 billion in the first year and $1.5 billion in the second year, just on the cost of parts. Right. I'd love to see that report. Who were they kidding? It never happened because there was absolutely no commonality between Mercedes and Chrysler at the manufacturing level. It didn't help that the Mercedes engineering and design operations flat-out refused to share their expertise with the crass Americans. The one joint venture the merger managed to cough up, a sporty car called the Crossfire, epitomized everything that was wrong with the deal from the Chrysler vantage point. The Crossfire was heralded as a cross between German design and American marketing. It was doomed from the start. Chrysler plants were in an uproar when they learned the car was being built in Germany, and who could blame them? This car wouldn't produce a single American job. Its arrival was a massive flop. Overpriced and underpowered, the

Crossfire bombed across America, selling fewer than fifty thousand units in three years.

It soon became obvious that this wasn't much of a merger. Schrempp really ran the show, and Eaton was silent. The old Chrysler management—the very people who were responsible for its success—began to leave or retire, one by one, taking their fat payouts with them. The management was mostly German. All news releases for the company were written in German and translated into English! Hard to believe. Half the time, the folks in Auburn Hills were scratching their heads, wondering, *What are they talking about?* A joke making the rounds at the time got it pretty right:

Q. How do you pronounce DaimlerChrysler?
A. Daimler. The Chrysler is silent.

Schrempp's assurances that it would be a "merger of equals" was about as likely as finding a marriage of equals in Saudi Arabia.

And what was Bob Eaton thinking? I'd say he was thinking something like, "How fast can I clean out my desk and get the hell out of here?" He basically took the money and ran. He retired in March 2000—a year short of his promised three years—saying his corporate goal had been reached. What was that corporate goal—to betray more than one hundred thousand American workers by turning over their proud, independent company to the Germans, while making himself rich? Call it a golden handshake or a golden parachute or a golden retirement. The point is, it was all golden for Eaton.

With Eaton's retirement, Schrempp dropped all pretense of the merger of equals, telling the London *Times*, "The Merger of Equals statement was necessary in order to earn the support of Chrysler's workers and the American public, but it was never reality."

When Schrempp's words reached Auburn Hills, the reaction was, "He didn't really say that, did he?" Nobody could believe it. When it sank in, they were dumbstruck. The merger was really a takeover. Eaton had to have known that from the start, but he let it happen. There are plenty of people who will never forgive him — starting with *me*.

Was anyone surprised when DaimlerChrysler started bleeding market share and dropping sales? By 2001, the company was worth about what Daimler-Benz alone had been worth at the time of the merger. Without being part of the S&P 500 Index, stockholders were bailing in droves, further driving down the share price. Its U.S. market share had plummeted from 16 percent to 13.5 percent. In 2001, Chrysler lost $2 billion and Mercedes lost $589 million.

After Eaton's flight and the firing of two American CEOs in succession, they finally got it right and found a great guy to run the company. Dieter Zetsche, the current German CEO of DaimlerChrysler, is the polar opposite of the rigid, autocratic Schrempp. After they put him in charge, he came to my house for dinner. He said he wanted to pick my brain. Well, that in itself was a good sign. Schrempp had liked to dictate orders. He hadn't been much for listening. I liked Dieter. With his big walrus mustache and his folksy manner, he came across as being very different from the usual Stuttgart crowd. I admired his honesty and knew quickly he was a good engineer and product man. Our conversation was very productive. We talked cars, engineer to engineer. I asked the gut questions—what were the problems, what were the first steps he was going to take? He demonstrated a real knowledge of cars and the car business, and I believed him when he said it was his mission to restore the company to its former greatness.

Dieter worked hard for three years, put together a good team, and won the respect of the American workers and the dealers. I give him a lot of credit for leadership. He succeeded in halting the downward spiral, but only briefly. As I write this, Chrysler is announcing huge layoffs, and there are rumors that Daimler is looking for a way to unload their American partner— maybe to *China*. Please, God, tell me this is a cruel joke. If Chrysler is kicked to the curb, it will be as a shattered remnant of the great American car company it once was. The seductive potential of the merger will have turned out to be nothing more than a mirage.

DOES BIGGER ALWAYS MEAN BETTER?

Why is everyone so merger-happy? There's a strange logic that's taken hold in the business world: When you're facing stiff competition, the best response is expansion. But that's not necessarily a winning strategy. When you stop to think about it, most of the great companies of our times began as upstarts—little Davids taking on big Goliaths. When I first heard about Fred Smith, the guy who created Federal Express, I thought the idea was crazy.

I remember thinking, He's going to take on the *post office?* Today Federal Express does such a huge business that even the U.S. Postal Service hires it to move a billion dollars in packages every year.

I had the same reaction when I heard about Jack Taylor's concept for Enterprise Rent-a-Car. I honestly didn't think he'd make it. His plan was to go up against the big boys—the Hertzes and Avises—with only one difference. Enterprise would pick customers up at their doors. Jack's slogan was "Pick Enterprise. We'll pick you up." Frankly, it didn't seem like a great enough incentive to get people to switch from their favorite companies. Shows you what I knew. Enterprise is now the *largest* car rental company in North America.

Here's another one. When Ted Turner told me he was planning to take on the three networks with a twenty-four-hour-a-day news channel, I said, "Come *on*, Ted, who's going to watch news twenty-four hours a day?" I thought CNN would last about six months. That was strike three for me!

These were three innovators on a small scale that turned into massive successes. There are plenty of examples of upstarts beating the giants, because the giants have become too fat and arrogant. They've stopped looking ahead. In 1943, Thomas Watson, the chairman of IBM, said, "I think there's a world market for maybe *five* computers." Okay, we can give Watson the benefit of the doubt; 1943 was a little bit early for computers. But it's hard to excuse Ken Olsen, the president and founder of Digital Equipment Corporation, who said in 1977, "There is no reason anyone would want a computer in their home." These Goliaths never saw it coming.

The lesson: Innovation can be much more important than size. Often, when companies get big they tend to grow sluggish. It takes a constant infusion of fresh ideas and leadership to prevent that.

TOO BIG FOR THEIR BRITCHES

Merger-mania hasn't just infected the auto industry. These days, everybody wants to merge. Too often they're just blindly gobbling up as many players as they can, in the false belief that bigger has to be better. It kind of makes you wonder if *merger*-mania isn't really just *ego*-mania. Or something even more destructive. If you look at it objectively, most mergers do not revitalize companies. Rather, they provide short-term gains for a relatively small group of people, usually Wall Street bankers and lawyers.

Look at the AOL–Time Warner merger in 2000. Everyone praised it as a brilliant marriage of old and new media. It lasted three years. The downfall of the AOL–Time Warner merger has sometimes been blamed on unexpected market forces—like the bursting of the Internet bubble. But the root cause of the failure was our old friend *synergy*—as in, there *was* none. It's hard to imagine Steve Case and his band of technology buffs in the hushed corridors of the stodgy old Time Warner building. Jerry Levin may have loved the idea of all that new technology, but he hadn't considered how he'd integrate his movie, TV, and magazine businesses with the Internet.

Lest you think I'm advocating a "small is beautiful" philosophy of business, let me assure you that the situation is more complex than just saying big is bad, small is good—or vice versa. The real choice isn't between big and small. It's between efficient and inefficient, profitable and unprofitable. That's where the ball gets dropped. Almost two thirds of all mergers fail to improve the value of the surviving entity's stock.

So, if the merger bug is buzzing around *your* company, here are a few things to look for:

Merger of equals? Don't fall for it. In my opinion, there is no such thing. Think about it. When have you ever seen a true merger of equals—in business or in life? Someone is always in the one-up position. If you don't believe me, think about your marriage. Can you honestly say it was a merger of complete equals? Usually one of the partners has an advantage. I think that's where the term "a good catch" comes from. Well, it's the same with businesses. As the saying goes, "All people are equal, but some are more equal than others." Proclaiming a merger of equals is usually just an attempt to put a good face on an acquisition.

It's all about synergy. The purpose of a merger is to create a stronger entity than each of the two parts. It's sort of a $1 + 1 = 3$ equation. The new entity should be leaner, more efficient, and more profitable. That can only happen if there's synergy. Now, it's easy for the top dogs to put on rose-colored glasses and imagine all the synergistic benefits of a merger. But it's a good idea to check with the line—the people who actually have to make it work. As DaimlerChrysler learned, synergy doesn't automatically exist just because you're in the same industry.

Don't forget the customer. At the start of a merger, while you're busy counting heads, cutting costs, and watching the stock market, don't let the important things slide—like meeting the needs of your customers. I don't care what kind of business you're in, if you lose the customers, you're dead.

Bigger can be better—but not always. There can definitely be advantages to bigness. But you have to beware of the deadly mentality that tends to creep into big organizations. Executives start thinking, "We've got it good. Why take any chances?" Well, the lessons of history should apply. Whether you're talking about the fall of Goliath, the fall of Rome, or the fall of IBM, there are just too many stories of the ambitious little guy overcoming the fat, sluggish big guy. If you're big, you've got to find a way to stay lively and creative.

When I was in business, I always believed that my legacy should be to make things better. In 1987 Chrysler had achieved a comeback and business was great. But I thought we were getting a little flabby around the middle. We needed a fresh infusion of creativity and a new challenge. I decided to buy American Motors, the venerable maker of the Jeep. When I put it to a vote among my top management, they voted it down. They couldn't understand why we'd mess with AMC when things were going so well.

Even my *mother* thought it was a lousy idea. "Why would you take on someone else's headaches?" she asked. "Why do you need that? Aren't things good enough?"

"Hey, Mom," I reminded her. "You know what Pop used to say: 'If you stand still, you'll go backward.'"

She didn't buy it, but I actually believed Pop was right. So I went ahead with the deal to acquire AMC. We paid half a billion in cash and some stock and earned $1 billion in the first year. The profit was gratifying, but more gratifying still was the renewed energy we felt. The acquisition kept us in fighting trim.

Merge because of your hopes, not your fears. It's a fact of life that when people or companies make decisions out of fear, they're already losing. There are a lot of fears driving corporate mergers these days—fear of globalization, fear of raiders, fear of the volatile stock market. But when you run a business based on fear you're no different than the animals in the jungle that act on the fight-or-flight instinct. Humans have brains—at least most of us do—and that means we can act based on reason and hope and possibility.

I don't pretend to know all the answers. Every business is unique. But I have a little quiz for any company that's considering a merger or an acquisition. It's just three questions:

Will it build a better mousetrap?
Will it ultimately create jobs?
Will it stand the test of time?
If you can answer YES to all three, go ahead and merge.

Otherwise, resist the urge.

XIV

Can anyone around here
run a car company?

I remember when Detroit really *meant* something to America. I'm not just talking about the economy. I'm talking about the future of democracy. Now, most of the people reading this book were not alive to hear Franklin D. Roosevelt herald Detroit as "the arsenal of democracy" during World War II, but those words made a lifelong impression on me. Even as a kid I felt such tremendous pride. Those were *our* factories, *our* workers, *our* determination to save the world. That was *our* arsenal building the combat vehicles and equipment that won World War II. When called to serve, Detroit responded. It was the American way—and it was a big reason I went into the car business.

Wouldn't it be something if Detroit could once again be the great arsenal of democracy? I don't mean building tanks. I mean saving our way of life and our communities. Remember, in World War II we took on Germany and Japan and we *beat* them—and then we *rebuilt* them. Now we must rebuild our own country. We must resurrect the hopes and dreams of the middle class.

In the 1980s, General Motors advertised Chevrolet as "the heartbeat of America." The slogan caught on, in part because it reflected the way we felt about our car industry. The pulse of America's Big Three was strong and steady. Detroit was the engine that drove our economy and the world. Today, the pulse is growing fainter. So what happened?

Well, for one thing, there *is* no American Big Three at the moment. After Chrysler became DaimlerChrysler, with decision-making coming out of Stuttgart, there were only the Big Two. Then Ford slipped behind Toyota in American car sales, and there was just the Big One—GM. With Toyota poised to overtake GM, I'm worried that we'll wake up one morning to read the headline, "And then there were none."

How did this happen? How did General Motors go from 60 percent of the market to 25 percent? How did Ford get out-paced by Toyota on its home turf? How did Chrysler come to press a panic button during its best sales year in history? And more important, what are these companies going to do now?

Times of crisis require bold moves, and this is where America has failed the great industry that created its prosperity. Last year the heads of GM, Ford, and Chrysler tried to meet with the President for months, and the White House kept canceling. Bush had time to meet with the winner of *American Idol*, but he couldn't squeeze in the leaders of the auto industry. Meanwhile, he was blowing them off in the press, saying things like,

"Detroit needs to learn how to compete," and "They have to start building a product that's relevant." Thanks a *lot,* Mr. President.

By the time Bush finally gave the CEOs forty-five minutes in late 2006, their agenda was pretty serious. The Big Three asked for help in three crucial areas that *require* government cooperation: the trade imbalance—especially Japan's manipulation of the yen and its closed markets; the health care crisis, for which the car companies bear an unfair burden; and the need to develop alternate fuels such as ethanol. The President's response was polite, but it was obvious he wasn't about to roll up *his* sleeves to help solve these problems. It was more like a photo op than a work session.

It's a good thing the industry doesn't have to depend solely on the executive branch for support. Now that my good friend Michigan congressman John Dingell is chairing the Committee on Energy and Commerce, auto manufacturers can count on a listening ear on Capitol Hill.

I can't believe I'm still talking about this almost twenty years after I accompanied the first President Bush to Japan to urge the Japanese to open their markets to U.S. products. In all this time what's happened is *nada, nothing, zip.* Twenty years later it's the same old song. No help with trade, no health care plan, no commitment to alternative energy.

When America needed the Big Three to be its arsenal of democracy, Detroit came through. Now, when Detroit asks the government to be its partner in revival, the White House gives it forty-five minutes.

Now, you might say to me, "A lot has changed since 1940,"

and you'd be right. But I don't believe that America is less capable of greatness than it was then. You'll never convince me that the spirit and genius we invested in *inventing* the greatest industry in the world can't be used to *reinvent* it. All it takes is the will to do it, and the leadership to set the course.

THE LEADERSHIP TO REBUILD

I get asked all the time, "Lee, if you were running a car company today, what would you do?" It's something I wonder about a lot. When you've spent your life in a business, it's hard not to play out the scenarios in your head, especially when the Big Three are constantly in the news.

So I'll take a stab at it. There is no question that the problems in Detroit are complex. But there are some basic steps *any* leader has to take if the American car industry is to survive. If you're faced with the challenge of heading up an American car company today, here are the things you *must* do:

Create a sense of urgency

You're up against the wall, and you're getting hammered. Instead of hiding in the corporate offices, get out there and communicate. Tell it like it is: "We have a tough task ahead of us. The challenges are formidable. But together we can do it. It'll take everyone—the employees, the dealers, the suppliers, the union, the government—and we're asking for your help."

Communication is the lubricant that makes an organization run—and never is that more true than during times of crisis. It always amazes me how big corporations will spend millions of dollars telling the public what's happening, but forget to tell their own employees. A good leader will make every person feel personally involved in the recovery. Many years ago, when Chrysler was fighting for its life, I went to every single plant so I could speak directly to the workers. I thanked them for hanging in there during those hard times, and I asked them to join me in restoring the company to greatness. There were a lot of cheers and some boos, but I got them involved.

If you haven't visited every plant this year, get out there and do it. Tell the workers what's happening, and enlist them in the fight. Meet with the plant supervisors and ask for their suggestions. Go to the dealers and the suppliers and hold strategy sessions: What should the priorities be? What should be cut? What should be changed?

Assemble a top team

The quality of your team will make or break your program. Remember, it's never just one person. Every so often, we get enamored of an individual, and start thinking that person is some kind of magician. Right now in the auto industry, that so-called boy wonder is a guy named Carlos Ghosn, who is credited with turning around Nissan, and he did a great job. But to say that Ghosn alone turned around Nissan is like saying that *I* alone turned around Chrysler. I brought eighty-eight guys with me from Ford—including a top management team. They helped save my ass. I guess what I'm saying is, there's not going to be a savior, just a team of seasoned leaders.

And make sure that team includes top talent in design, engineering, and manufacturing, because that's your *only* priority—to build cars people want to buy. Hot styling still sells them, but quality keeps them sold.

When I was head of Chrysler, I couldn't walk into a plant and instantly see whether it was running efficiently or not. But I had people who could—notably Dick Dauch and Steve Sharf, who were my secret weapons in manufacturing and brought real quality to our products in a short period of time.

Share the sacrifice

In the coming months and years, you're going to have to make more painful choices. Not everyone will survive, and those who do will have to take a haircut and maybe a shave, too. You must demonstrate equality of sacrifice. When you ask everyone to join the cause, you'll get no cooperation if the workers are grumbling, "Why am I taking a beating? The fat cats are up there earning millions, and you want to cut my *what?*"

We saved Chrysler for one reason. Everyone shared in the sacrifice—starting with me. You see, it wouldn't have gone down too well if I'd asked the rank and file to tighten their belts while I was putting extra notches in mine. So I cut my salary to one dollar a year. That is an example of leadership, born in a crisis. Then I went to the executives and asked them to take a pay cut. Finally, I went to Doug Fraser of the UAW and asked what the union could give. The workers really came through. Over a nineteen-month period, the workers made $2.5 billion in concessions. It was the workers more than the government loan that saved the company.

Simplify!

It's time to get back to basics. There are too many models, and you have to get rid of some of them. The complexity of your product lines is killing you. Remember, Toyota only has three brands—its nameplate Toyota, Lexus, and a funky little car called the Scion.

I know this is a controversial idea, but you need to retire the Sloan model. Alfred Sloan was a genius in his day. Back in the 1920s, he had a vision that took hold of the nation. A car for everyone. Not just the elite, but ordinary people, too. Sloan's vision was so effective that even during the height of the Depression, President Herbert Hoover defined the American birthright as "a chicken in every pot and a car in every garage."

Sloan's model of a car for every income level motivated people to trade upward as they progressed in life. In other words, you started with a Chevy and were buried in a Cadillac hearse. Sloan's brand concept built GM into a powerhouse, and Ford and Chrysler followed suit. But the Sloan model just doesn't work anymore. Your companies are being smothered by a glut of brands and models within a brand. GM, in particular, is saddled with an unwieldy breadth of market. Does every brand really need a minivan, a big SUV, a little SUV, a crossover, a station wagon, a two-door coupe, a four-door sedan, and a convertible? That's just plain crazy. It confuses the customers, kills the dealers, and plays havoc with assembly plants, making it almost impossible to build a production schedule to meet market demand.

American car companies need a new, leaner rule of the road that builds brand identity and allows them to streamline the manufacturing process. It would be nice if you could always utilize plants to full capacity, but that's hard to do these days. A plant's optimum capacity is about 250,000 vehicles a year, and there aren't too many models with that instant appeal anymore. So an efficient plant has to be able to build up to five models of about 50,000 each—and that means commonality of parts. I've been impressed by Chrysler's new flexible manufacturing plan that allows them to do just that. Their robots are amazing. You can change the hands on a robot and build an entirely different car. Now, that's *real* innovation.

Shuck the losers

Make a list of the three most profitable brands—at the factory level and at the dealer level. Then take the three or so least profitable brands and give them one year to break even. If they can't get into the black, drop them.

Car companies—like all other big bureaucracies—have a real aversion to giving up on something once they've poured a ton of cash into it. There's always an attitude that success is just around the corner. I hate to say it, but it's time to *cut and run* on some of these products. I give GM high marks for dropping Oldsmobile a couple of years ago. It must have been an agonizing decision. Here was a brand that had been around for over one hundred years, but GM rightly determined it was time to end Oldsmobile's run.

After making such a tough decision with Oldsmobile, closing Saturn should be a no-brainer. Saturn was a mistake to begin with when Roger Smith first imagined building his Japan-beating small car, and the mistake keeps growing. I've heard that Saturn has never turned a profit in its thirteen-year life. You have to ask: What is the franchise that GM is protecting?

Ford's recent mistakes have been costly, and its identity crisis has been demoralizing. I've never understood why Ford needed to acquire nameplates like Jaguar, Volvo, Aston Martin, and Land Rover. Sometimes I look at Ford and I feel like asking, "What do you want to be when you grow up?" Ford thought it could buy its way into the luxury car market. It didn't work.

Off the top, Jaguar's got to go. Ford has poured over $5 billion into Jaguar, and it's *still* in the red. Another money loser is Land Rover. Finally—and this is the hardest—you need to evaluate whether Mercury can be profitable and have some identity in the market.

Follow the market

During my years in the car industry, we hit two out of the ballpark—the Mustang at Ford and the minivan at Chrysler. The formula for their success was a departure from the original Sloan model of a car for every purse. These vehicles were built for lifestyles.

The Mustang was a big success because it was a lifestyle car for baby boomers. In 1964 they were teenagers with their first driver's licenses. They craved mobility. And they (or I should say their *parents*) had the disposable income to afford it. They responded to the Mustang because it was a beauty, it had power, and it had an identity. It became a cult car. To this day, when I go to the classic Mustang shows, those now-aging baby boomers treat me like a rock star. That car *meant* something to them.

In the 1980s, our big success was the minivan. We'd followed the baby boomers, and they'd grown up, married, moved to the suburbs, and acquired a couple of kids and a dog. The minivan spoke to that lifestyle—and, by the way, it still does. Twenty-two years later, with not much competition, Chrysler is still selling 30,000 minivans a month. I guess soccer moms are still alive and kicking.

You cannot lose if you follow the market.

For much of its history the American auto industry took an ass-backward approach to the market. They basically said, "We'll decide which cars to build, and then we'll try to convince people that they want and need them." Then someone came up with a bright idea: "Why don't we find out what kind of cars the customers want and need, and then build them?" It's *still* a bright idea.

The best situation in the world is when dealers are beating down your doors for a car because their customers are beating down *their* doors for a car. You don't just roll them off the line and hope you can find a way to get rid of them.

Lighten up

It's about time we stopped promoting the fiction that bigger, heavier vehicles deliver more safety on the road. America went crazy over the SUV because people believed all that iron protected them. Here's the truth: You don't make cars safer by just adding weight. Study after study has shown that weight alone doesn't protect drivers.

When I bought Jeep, I predicted a market for SUVs of about half a million vehicles. I thought it might be a *niche* market, or even a fad. I didn't realize it was the start of something big—a whole new class of vehicles. If you'd told me that in just twenty years about every brand in the world would need an SUV, and that annual sales would get to the five million mark, I would have said you were crazy. But the SUV is a phenomenon.

The question is, why has the SUV been such a success? What is its purpose in life? Very few people go off-road, so it's not because they need a rugged all-terrain vehicle. The SUV doesn't have the passenger or storage capacity of a minivan, or the good ride and handling of a car.

So, what is the motivation for buying an SUV? Why are we lugging around all that extra weight? Bigger engines (usually V-8s) are not known for fuel economy and low emissions.

I think the SUV feeds a strong desire for security

and control on the road. In this day and age, people want to put as much steel and iron around them as they can. They equate weight with safety. It's a factor, but in no way compares to solid structural design and the use of multiple air bags. I think people are looking for a competitive edge on the freeway and they like riding high in a command position behind the wheel. With thousands of other SUVs speeding past them, not to mention eighteen-wheelers and cement mixers, drivers just *feel* more secure. It's a perception and Detroit promoted it. One SUV brand advertised itself with the headline, "Look upon it as a 4,000-pound security blanket."

It might be kind of a macho thing, too. The introduction of the 1990 Jeep Grand Cherokee kick-started the whole market and coincided with Desert Storm and those huge wartime Humvees. They evolved into Hummers for home consumption. Hummers are the ultimate example of the bigger-is-safer mentality: If you want guaranteed safety on the road, why not drive a *tank*!

The oil crisis of the 1970s was a wake-up call: Start to build smaller cars, or die. Well, we got a late start on that, behind our Japanese competitors, but once we started to build smaller cars, we got pretty good at it. Eventually, gas prices leveled off, and we started forgetting the pain of the long gas lines of the 1970s. Maybe we thought gas prices would stay low forever. We began building bigger, heavier vehicles.

Today we've reached another period of instability with energy prices, and we've got to get smarter this time around.

The market imperative is so clear you'd have to be blind not to see it. We need to build more small cars. Right now, *none* of the smallest cars are built by Detroit.

We need to spend more R&D on hybrids. And we need to do it aggressively. I'm not talking about sticking a toe in the water with the development of crossover vehicles. What the hell is a crossover vehicle? It's an SUV on a car chassis that will probably never go off-road. It's smaller than a minivan. Well, let me see . . . that would be a . . . CAR! Stop building models that people don't need, and concentrate on a lean, strong product program.

Detroit has been shamefully late getting into hybrid development. The excuse: Hybrids are not yet as fuel efficient as they should be, and they're expensive to build. We need to exert some creativity here, or we'll be ceding the future market to Honda and Toyota.

Lock the Big Three in a room

By the "Big Three" I mean the *companies*, the *union*, and the *government*. There *must* be across-the-board collaboration to make this comeback work.

As this book goes to press, the UAW is gearing

up for a major contract showdown in September 2007. There are a lot of big-ticket issues on the table, and this negotiation is going to require some major leadership.

Here's the way I see it. There's a lot of talk these days about whether we live in a *faith-based* world or a *reality-based* world. Well, I think this discussion is relevant for the unions. In a *faith-based* world, the UAW throws its hands to the heavens and says, "GM [or Ford or Chrysler] will provide." In a *reality-based* world, the UAW understands that the burdens of legacy costs have the automakers fighting for their lives. In a *reality-based* world, the UAW sees that companies like Toyota are thriving by building nonunion factories. In a *reality-based* world, the UAW realizes that Ford and GM have already taken the first shots across their bows with massive employee buyout plans. More than 65,000 workers are taking the buyout money from these two companies and leaving the industry. Two great companies are being hollowed out of skilled workers. It's madness. Where do you think those workers are going to go? They're not all retiring. They might even take their skills to Toyota, which would be the ultimate irony.

As for the government, well, if the auto industry really *is* the heartbeat of America, someone had better warn the government that the old ticker is on life support. The lukewarm interest of the Bush administration has been demoralizing.

When Chrysler was sliding into bankruptcy, and I was trying to sell Washington on the idea of a loan, I raised this question with Congress: *Would America be better off without Chrysler?* Now, you've got to understand that there was huge resistance in Washington and on Wall Street to a bailout for Chrysler. All those free enterprise purists had their noses in the air. They defined free enterprise as survival of the fittest, as if we were playing some kind of ancient caveman's game. I had to show them it was in their interest to keep Chrysler solvent.

I did it with numbers. The Treasury Department had estimated that if Chrysler collapsed it would cost the country $2.7 billion during the first year alone in unemployment insurance and welfare payments. I said to Congress, "You guys have a choice. Do you want to pay the $2.7 billion now, or do you want to guarantee loans of half that amount with a good chance of getting it all back? You can pay now or you can pay later." That made people sit up and take notice.

Then, with the help of my friend Speaker of the House Tip O'Neill, I broke it down for each congressman. I think there were only two districts in America that didn't have a Chrysler dealer or supplier providing jobs. So I put it to them in terms each representative could understand: If Chrysler went under, their district would lose jobs. And I told them just how many. It worked because they came to see a loan for Chrysler as a way to save jobs in *their* neighborhoods.

Maybe you're thinking, *There he goes again, angling for bailouts.* I'm not talking about bailouts. I'm talking about the government understanding that it has a stake in the success of the auto industry. I'm talking about the government agreeing that it has an obligation to help level the playing field.

Look at it this way: The *acronyms* are killing us. There's OPEC (the Organization of Petroleum Exporting Countries), which has been around for thirty-six years, controlling the oil spigot at the whim of the cartel. There's MITI (Japan's Ministry of International Trade and Industry), which has been around for sixty years, manipulating currency in a way that would be illegal if it were happening in America. And there's UAW (United Auto Workers), which has been around for seventy-five years, playing the *gimmie* game with every new contract. Whenever you see an acronym, you know you're in trouble. And isn't it a bit much to expect one executive—or even *three* executives—to take on these long-established and entrenched organizations?

American carmakers have struggled to stay competitive in spite of being saddled with the kinds of burdens the foreign competition never has to worry about—such as skyrocketing pension and health care costs, intractable unions, government regulations, and a growing trade imbalance. All of these factors translate into brutal fixed costs on the production of cars, and a constant scramble for capital. Our Japanese and European competitors essentially have a blank check from either government-owned or highly regulated banks. (For years the going interest rate from the Bank of Japan has been 0–1 percent, if you can believe that!) Year after year our trade representatives sit around eating sushi and making nice with the Japanese, and never push for a level playing field. Meanwhile, our state governments treat the Japanese auto companies like conquering heroes.

Here's an example. A newly built Toyota plant in San Antonio, Texas, has become the darling of the state. They've showered Toyota with millions of dollars of incentives, worth about $600 per car. And that's not even the best part for Toyota. Its young workforce is nonunion. There is virtually no burden of pension and health care costs. Meanwhile, a couple hundred miles down the road, a thirty-year-old GM plant in Arlington—one of the company's most successful—doesn't get any of the red carpet treatment, but it gets *all* of the headaches. And the biggest headache of all is health care. GM pays $1,525 per vehicle for health care to Toyota's $201.

Our government ignores the very real and looming crisis of legacy costs at its own risk. How about some incentives for the companies that are keeping retirees solvent? How about a health care plan that won't bankrupt industry? General Motors is the largest private purchaser of health care in the United States, offering coverage to 1.1 million people. Twenty years ago at Chrysler, I was shocked to learn that Goodyear Tire and U.S. Steel weren't our biggest suppliers—Blue Cross/Blue Shield was. Today it's even worse. And it's not just the auto industry that's affected. Howard Schultz, the chairman of Starbucks, says his company spends more on health insurance than it spends on coffee beans! What do you think would happen if all of those people were suddenly uninsured? That is a question a responsible government needs to address.

Leadership in the car industry means knowing when corporate policy ends and public policy begins. You see, companies are not separate entities from government. Everyone has a part to play in the recovery of our manufacturing sector. But it will take real leadership in the "Big Three" of corporation-union-government to get it done.

WHO WILL LEAD?

I've said before that leadership is born in times of crisis, and Detroit has got a hell of a crisis on its hands. The question is, What kind of leaders are emerging from this crisis?

Here, I have to say, the news is actually very good.

At GM, Rick Wagoner has exhibited amazing cool in the face of a serious arm-twisting by Kirk Kerkorian, Jerry York, and Carlos Ghosn. They pushed a merger with Renault-Nissan that would have solved exactly *none* of GM's problems. Kerkorian and York, as I mentioned earlier, know how to play those high-stakes poker games, but Wagoner didn't fold. Instead, in his low-key, under-the-radar way, he showed the merger specialists to the door, and has instituted a new drive for improved product design, with the help of a savvy veteran, Bob Lutz.

Chrysler's Tom LaSorda may be just the guy the company needs for a back-to-basics drive to reverse its slump. As a former factory boss (and the son and grandson of labor leaders), LaSorda understands the nuts and bolts of the business. He also has the ability to inspire trust among the workers. When he says, "I know what you're experiencing," he means it.

It's too early to know how Ford's new chief, former Boeing executive Bill Mulally, will adapt to the car industry. Sometimes an outsider's perspective can reenergize a tired business plan. I will say one thing about the leadership change. Bill Ford earns my admiration for stepping up and acknowledging the crisis — and admitting that maybe he was in a little over his head and needed help. His move took a lot of guts.

A leader in the auto industry has to have a passion for cars and an enthusiasm for innovation. The leader sets the tone for the entire company, and when I was CEO I always wanted my tone to communicate that we could do great things together. I hope the current leaders feel that way, too. Wouldn't it be something if the best days of America's arsenal of democracy were still ahead of us?

XV

Who will save
the middle class?

I've been looking for the middle class, and I have to admit that I'm having a hard time finding it. No one seems to know how to define it. A lot of economists say that the middle class is a state of mind. Well, that doesn't seem right. When I read the newspapers, they talk about the *Middle Class Vote*, and the *Middle Class Financial Crunch*, and the *Middle Class Health Care Crisis*. They talk about the *Middle Class Losing Jobs to Globalization*, and the *Middle Class Tax Burden*, and the *Middle Class Credit Card Debt*. That doesn't sound like a state of mind to me. We're talking about real people here. But who are they?

Even the middle class has trouble defining itself. When pollsters ask people if they consider themselves middle class, they get "yes" answers from those who have income levels anywhere between $20,000 and $100,000. Obviously, you can't pin it down based solely on income. There are too many variables—

like where you live, the size of your family, and whether or not your job has benefits.

When I think of the middle class, what comes to mind are the hardworking people I've known in my life who have dreams and aspirations for themselves and their children. I grew up in that kind of family. Like most immigrants, my parents believed in the American dream: Anything was possible if you worked hard and got a good education. They made sure our family always had a roof over its head and plenty of good home-cooked food on the table. My parents knew how to stretch a nickel, and we never wanted for the important things—even during the Depression. We always had everything we needed, and then some.

It never occurred to my dad that I wouldn't do better than he did in life. He was always teaching me, always imparting lessons. He wasn't surprised that I prospered. He expected it. When I became president of Ford, the first call I made was to my wife, and the second was to my father in Allentown, Pennsylvania. He was eighty years old, and he'd seen a lot in his life, but this was one of his high points.

It's been a long time since I was a member of the middle class. I'm not going to pretend that I experience the stresses and strains or feel the pinch that is a way of life for most Americans. But I'll tell you one thing. I've never stopped appreciating the hopes and aspirations of the middle class. That was my father's legacy. I got where I am through the grace of God, a little talent, hard work, a lot of luck, and because I lived in the land of opportunity. And I've always wanted to see others have the same chance.

America needs the middle class. You can't run a country with just the very rich and the very poor. The middle class keeps the economy rolling. As long as a family is making enough to meet its mortgage payments, eat fairly well, have two cars in the garage, send a kid to college, go out once a week for dinner and a movie, and have a little extra left over, they're fairly content. We used to talk about "Joe Lunchbucket." I guess now it's Soccer Mom and NASCAR Dad. But the reality is the same.

The middle class has been called "the silent majority." But it hasn't been so silent lately, because people are scared. I have to say I've never before seen this level of anxiety from working people.

CAN UNIONS SAVE THE MIDDLE CLASS?

The middle class may be hard to define, but it's not an abstraction to me. I spent my life in the auto industry, and you can make a good argument that the auto industry *created* the middle class. Henry Ford took the first step. Way back in 1914, before there were industrial labor unions, Ford did a smart thing. He figured out that the best way to motivate employees was to give them a stake in success—and that meant a living wage and a reasonable workday. He shortened the workday from nine hours to eight, and raised the minimum wage from $2.34 to $5 a day. In spite of his critics—mostly from Wall Street—Ford's idea worked. Profits soared, and for the first time the workers in his plants could also afford to become his customers. He once said, "The payment of five dollars for an eight-hour day was one of the finest cost-cutting moves we ever made."

Of course, Henry Ford wasn't being purely altruistic. Part

of Ford's goal was to block efforts to unionize his plants. He always said that his company would unionize over his dead body, and it almost came to that. Ford was the last automaker to let the UAW in.

Now, there are plenty of people who would say that the unions built the middle class in the twentieth century, and there's some truth to that. Unionized workers didn't have to depend on the paternalistic instincts of owners like Ford. The rights and dignity of the worker were upheld through fair wages, safe work environments, adequate health care, insurance for old age or disability, reasonable work schedules, and time off. It was a pretty radical idea, when you think about it. Through unions, ordinary working men and women could join together to exert real power. They could get a fair shake.

Walter Reuther, who founded the UAW, was one of the clear leaders of the twentieth century. I met him once, and I always regretted that I never had a chance to get to know him better. He died in a plane crash shortly after I became president of Ford. He was a powerful speaker and a brilliant negotiator. Reuther had a gift for putting things simply. He always said that labor's task came down to one thing: carving up the pie as fairly as possible. And the bigger the pie, the bigger the slice for the workers.

I was told that Reuther would actually sit down at negotiating sessions and draw a picture of a pie. He'd divide the pie into slices, showing how much of it was going for raw materials, overhead, executive salaries, and labor. Then he'd tell them: "We're not satisfied with our slice"—and he'd show them how he wanted to cut the pie differently.

In a sense, the labor unions were *too* successful in the decades after World War II. They kept upping the ante, and we all went along because we had the cash and we were terrified of strikes. We set in motion the automatic cost-of-living allowance (COLA), which was adopted by industries across America. We caved in to the union proposal of "thirty and out," which stipulated that after a worker had been on the payroll for thirty years, he or she was free to retire early, no matter how old, with a full pension. Now, *you* do the math: Say a worker starts at age eighteen. Thirty years puts him or her at the creaky old age of forty-eight. What were we thinking? It was one bonanza after another for labor. We gave away the store, and the UAW just asked for more. Nobody was planning for what might happen if times got tough—which they did. The automakers were forced to close plants and lay off workers in huge numbers. It's still happening today.

The "jobs bank" is a perfect example of an asinine concession the automakers made to the UAW in the 1980s. The jobs bank arranged to give workers who got laid off due to new technology, plant restructuring, or outsourcing full salaries for doing *nothing*, until such a time—maybe *never*—when they would be called back to work. Today, there are still over ten thousand workers sitting around playing cards or watching TV on company time. Does this make any sense?

The glory days of the UAW are over, and that's true for most unions. Today in the private sector, labor unions represent only 11 percent of manufacturing workers, and their membership continues to dwindle. Why? Well, a basic premise of business also applies to the unions: If you're filling a need, you'll do well. If you're not filling a need, you'll die. The unions haven't changed with the times. They haven't reinvented themselves to meet the new challenges of a global workforce and a global marketplace. Like many organizations that start out with high ideals, the unions have become too politicized and have lost some of their relevance. The question is, Can they get it back?

THE MIDDLE-CLASS FEAR

I talk to a lot of people in the course of a year. For one thing, wherever I go people come up to me and tell me about their dads who worked in a Ford plant, or their uncles who were Chrysler dealers, or their brothers who lost their jobs to plant closings. If I'm in a restaurant, there are always people coming over to shake my hand, to reminisce, to thank me for saving somebody's job thirty years ago, or to give me a piece of their mind. There aren't too many happy faces these days. Everybody is worried.

I've been hearing plenty of sad stories, and, yes, a lot of anger, too. I can understand that. When you've worked all your life in a company, with the promise that you can retire with a pension and health care benefits, it's a devastating betrayal when the company doesn't hold up its end of the bargain. The average guy just doesn't understand how this can happen, especially when he sees the guys at the top raking in unimaginable riches.

But the thing that scares people the most is health care. It used to be just the working poor who couldn't afford health insurance, but now that the price tag for the average family has reached almost $12,000 a year, it's affecting the entire middle class. Today, 46 million Americans have no health insurance at all.

If you're going to be outraged about the lack of leadership in this country, health care is a good place to start. The situation is getting worse every year, and nobody's doing a damn thing about it. The last time Washington even *looked* at health care was back in 1993 with Hillary Clinton's task force. We all know what a disaster Hillary's plan was—but hey, folks, that was *fourteen years* ago. Since then, nothing. The folks in Washington basically said, "Your plan is lousy so let's just forget about it."

It's a scandal, and we're letting it happen.

The burden of health care can single-handedly wipe out the middle class. All it takes is one medical crisis to drop a family from comfortably middle class to poor. It can happen overnight. You have a complicated labor, and suddenly you're looking at $25,000 for a C-section. Your kid breaks a leg playing soccer, and it's an $8,000 trip to the emergency room. Bypass surgery after a heart attack: $40,000. No wonder people are scared. And it's not just the uninsured. Workers are paying an increasing percentage of health insurance costs in industries where companies just can't afford to foot the whole bill anymore. With job security in the manufacturing sector at an all-time low, millions of workers are just a pink slip away from losing their health benefits. This is a solution that cries out for government leadership.

A PLAN FOR REVIVAL

Twenty-three years ago, in my first book, *Iacocca*, I proposed that we establish something comparable to a Marshall Plan for U.S. industry. I even had a name for it—the Critical Industries Commission. It would provide a setting for government, labor, and management to find a way out of the mess we were in. It would require collaboration. It would also require equality of sacrifice. Everyone would have to give up something for the good of all. Then the commission could get down to the business of figuring out how to strengthen our homegrown industries. In Japan and China, they protect their vital industries to a *fault*. Can't we make an effort to meet each other in the middle for the good of the nation?

Well, as you probably guessed, nobody took me up on my idea. And here we are, all these years later, much worse off than we were then. So I'll give it another shot. Look, if the United States could establish the Marshall Plan to rebuild Europe after World War II, and if we could establish the International Monetary Fund to help rebuild the world, and if we can spend a trillion dollars trying to rebuild Iraq, why can't we do the same thing for our country today? This isn't charity; it's necessity. It's self-interest. Did we rebuild Europe because we were playing Mr. Nice Guy? No, we rebuilt Europe because we had an interest in a strong Europe.

You have to face the problems head-on while they're happening, or they build up and become catastrophes. Sometimes I think our government and even some of our business leaders believe that if they just ignore the crisis in the middle class, every-thing will eventually work out.

The middle class is useful to politicians during election sea-son, when the slogans are flying. It doesn't matter if it's Democ-rats or Republicans. *Everyone* presents themselves as champions of the middle class when they're trolling for votes. They love to shake hands at the factory gates, but once they get to Washing-ton they can't be bothered with helping to keep those gates open. That's why we need permanent solutions like the Critical Indus-tries Commission.

THE NEW AMERICAN DREAM

I've often been asked to give graduation speeches at colleges and universities. Graduations are happy occasions. You look out on those faces and it's really uplifting to think these kids have their whole futures ahead of them. But in recent years I've had to wonder how bright those futures will be.

When I graduated from Lehigh University in 1946, I already had about twenty offers for employment. I started my first job at Ford the year after World War II ended. Harry Tru-man was President, and the world felt full of optimism. I remember thinking if only I could earn $10,000 a year I'd be sat-isfied. I couldn't wait to get started.

Today we need a new American dream that reflects the hopes and aspirations of the next generation. Let's give some thought to what that dream might be. Can you think of a polit-ical leader who's articulating it? Has anyone made you feel excited lately about the possibilities that are in store for your children and grandchildren? Nations aren't built on rhetoric, but they start with good ideas. In the coming election season, there will be a lot of pandering to the middle class. Let's make a commitment to cut through the bullshit and listen for the plan of action that has a chance of working. Let's be the adults in the room, and do it for our kids.

XVI

The blame game
is killing us

It occurs to me that one reason we're having so much trouble competing in the global economy is that we're spending too much time, energy, and money fighting with each other in *this* country.

America has the distinction of being the most litigious society on earth. We sue each other at the drop of a hat—or at the drop of a hot cup of coffee. About 90 percent of all civil actions tried before juries in the whole world are tried right here in the U.S.A.

Our courts are jammed, and it's no wonder, because so many people are looking to the courts not just to dispense justice, but to redistribute wealth. I don't think that's what the framers of the Constitution had in mind when they gave us our wonderful system of justice.

Some of the wacky lawsuits you read about are pretty funny. Like the burglar who fell through the skylight and tried to collect damages from the owners; or the college students who sued their school because they'd been promised a course would be easy and it was hard. These stories belong in *Ripley's Believe It or Not*. They are more of a distraction than anything else.

It's the serious lawsuits with awards in the millions and even billions that choke you up. They have squeezed decent companies dry, frozen competition, and cost the taxpayers countless billions in the costs of running civil courts.

TAKING RISKS ON THE ROAD TO SUCCESS

America's ability to compete is directly tied to the lawsuit frenzy. You see, the first thing you have to do in order to compete is take a risk. If you can't afford to take a risk, you can't afford to compete. As Americans, we've always pictured ourselves as daring and entrepreneurial, but today we've grown so litigation-obsessed that nobody wants to take risks anymore.

There used to be eighteen companies making football helmets in this country, but now hardly anyone does. Too risky. Maybe they're a little unnerved by what happened to Riddell Sports. After an eighteen-year-old boy suffered brain injury during a football game, his parents sued the helmet manufacturer for damages, and won $14.62 million. They never actually proved that the helmet was defective. In fact, the medical experts suggested it was a preexisting brain condition. But the jury handed over the money anyway.

We've virtually stopped making light aircraft in America. The biggest production cost is the liability insurance.

One of these days we're going to wake up and say, "The hell with it. Competing is just too risky."

Meanwhile, the competition is killing us. Other countries don't spend their time looking for Mr. Deep Pockets. They're too busy beating our brains out in the marketplace. The biggest damage award ever in the history of Great Britain was a little over a million bucks. That's practically a nuisance suit over here!

The Japanese don't even bother with court. They've got about as many lawyers in Japan as we've got Sumo wrestlers here.

Without competition, you don't have innovation. Forget about progress. Nowhere is this clearer than in health care. If you're a drug company, you might not want to mess around with actually finding a cure for a common disease. Too risky. Ask Merck. Conservative estimates put the litigation potential for Vioxx, the popular arthritis drug that may have triggered heart attacks in a few users, at $50 billion.

And forget about developing a new vaccine for, say, avian flu. Why get into that can of worms (no pun intended)? Vaccines are particularly vulnerable to litigation, so if you're a drug company, you might decide to spend your R&D budget on something safer—like growing hair (although you might be in trouble if the hair grew on a guy's feet instead of his head).

The real cost of litigation is that new doctors are avoiding certain important specialties—obstetrics, neurology, emergency room—like the plague. Insurance costs too much.

You might be thinking, Well what do you expect from a guy who spent his life in the car business? But I'm not averse to all litigation. If a company or individual has been negligent or has shown reckless disregard for safety, he should pay for it. But I'm afraid that we've reached a point where we're not just punishing gross negligence. We're punishing people who take normal risks that can't be avoided when you produce almost any kind of product.

When we do that, we're punishing ourselves. We're wrecking our ability to compete. We're stomping out progress.

REVENGE IS NOT SO SWEET

Punitive damages are the place where lawsuits really go overboard. It's one thing to compensate victims for their physical and monetary losses, but punitive damages are out of control. Juries get swept up in the emotions of a trial, and before you know it they're writing fifty-million-dollar checks.

With punitive damages, people can get awards up to triple their damages, based on a very subjective notion of pain and suffering. Most of the world has never even heard of punitive damages. It's a very American idea. So is the system of contingency fees in big civil action cases, which allows lawyers to win the lottery when their clients collect. It's an insane system, and when people talk about tort reform, they're talking about bringing it back into a zone of reality—applying some common sense to the way compensation is awarded. This is very hard for Americans to grasp, because we're seduced by big jackpots.

Maybe the real issue is what we value as a society. Why do we find it so easy and satisfying to hand over staggering amounts of money to a single individual who has suffered pain or loss, but hold back when it comes to showing compassion toward a community upended by natural disaster or economic blight?

It's something to think about.

NO-FAULT LIVING

There's such a thing as being too safety conscious. I remember some years ago being at a party at the home of Lee Annenberg, wife of the late publisher Walter Annenberg. I was seated at a table with Lady Sarah Ferguson, who was then married to Prince Andrew. At one point, Fergie jumped up and said, "This party is pretty *dull*. Let's dance." I'd never danced with a duchess before, so I said I'd be delighted. Fergie and I started to jitterbug to a fast number when all of a sudden a very British-looking guy came out of nowhere and tapped me on the shoulder. At first I thought he was cutting in, but he said, "Sir, I am Lady Ferguson's traveling gynecologist and she is with child. If you must dance, please do so by sliding your feet gently across the floor, rather than bouncing the lady up and down."

I gaped at him, but Fergie just gave him an annoyed look and said, "Hey, why don't you buzz off?" We kept on dancing, but at a slower pace. I didn't want to be party to creating an international incident.

Later, I laughed at how excessively cautious the Brits were. I'm sure Fergie gave her keepers heart failure many times. She wasn't a "safety first" kind of girl.

But the truth is, we don't live in a risk-free world, and we never will. We're mere mortals, and, yes, bad things *do* happen to good people. We get sick. We have accidents. We are disappointed. Things don't always work the way they're supposed to. So, what do we do? We look for someone to blame. The new American way is: "If something bad happens, somebody has to pay."

There was a time not that long ago when we were more civil. We gave people the benefit of the doubt. We tried to work out our differences face-to-face, not through lawyers. We'd tell people to "have a nice day." Now we say, "I'll see you in court."

It's not just our ability to compete that gets harmed by all the litigation. It's our ability to live with one another, to help each other out in bad times, to cooperate because we want to and because it's the right thing to do—not because we might get sued.

I've had a lot of time to contemplate this matter, having spent my career in the car industry. Automobile-related damages account for half of all the civil lawsuits in this country, and for half of all the compensations paid. Whenever there's a serious accident, the automakers end up with a liability suit, whether the *car* had anything to do with it or not.

I spent most of my career trying to find ways to make cars safer. I was involved in creating the interlock seat belt system. If your seat belt wasn't hooked up, the car wouldn't start. The House of Representatives shot that down in a hurry. They thought it was too intrusive on the part of the federal government. But at least every state now has some kind of law mandating seat belt use.

Cars today are built for safety. Not just the air bags, rollover bags, and crush zones, but also the way steering wheels are designed with controls at your fingertips. We decided that when you're driving a four-thousand-pound piece of iron at fifty to seventy-five miles an hour, it's a good idea to keep your hands on the wheel. Which, by the way, Californians notoriously don't do. As Red Buttons once said, "All you need to qualify for a driver's license out here is a middle finger."

But the greatest safety challenge of all is changing the way people behave when they're behind the wheel. And what really gets me about all the litigation is that it takes the idea of personal responsibility right off the table.

In 1980, when I was new at Chrysler, a woman named Candi Lightner started an organization called Mothers Against Drunk Driving (MADD). Candi's thirteen-year-old daughter had been mowed down by a drunk driver while walking down a country road. Candi was devastated by the death of her daughter, but when Candi found out that half of all fatalities were caused by drunk drivers, she was, well, *mad.* Candi's organization, MADD, has saved hundreds of thousands of lives since its start.

Now I'd like to see another organization formed. Let's call it Mothers Against *Distracted* Driving. Distraction is what kills people on the road today.

Morning drive time can be hazardous to your health. You've got someone in a five-thousand-pound SUV, juggling a hot cup of coffee, while using the vanity mirror to apply lipstick. You've got someone else in a four-thousand-pound sedan jabbering on a cell phone while lighting a cigarette. You've got a third person in a three-thousand-pound minivan trying to read the instructions on the navigation system, while catching the morning scream-fest on talk radio and the sibling scream-fest in the backseat. And someone else is zipping in and out of traffic in a sporty coupe, while getting stock quotes on his cell phone and eating an egg sandwich.

Is anyone watching the *road*?

I know that Mothers Against Distracted Driving would be a hard sell. People don't like interference. I also admit that I inadvertently contributed to the distraction problem by designing the first cupholders and driver-side vanity mirrors.

Of course, I realize that there's no test for distraction like there is for alcohol, so it would be kind of hard to enforce any kind of regulations. But maybe car companies could limit the technology a bit. Just because it's possible to hook up video screens in cars, it doesn't mean we have to do it. I'd like to propose that we strictly limit *all* video in the front seat.

Regulations only go so far. We could all vow, on our own, without a single law, to get behind the wheel, place our hands at the two o'clock and ten o'clock positions, face forward, eyes on the road—and drive with all due respect for that big hunk of iron. We can do it for ourselves, and for our children, and for the countless strangers whose paths we cross. Respect for others, responsibility for ourselves and others—these are basic tenets of a civilized society. Why don't we take them out for a spin?

PART FOUR

CAN AMERICA
BE GREAT AGAIN?

XVII

Are we too fat and satisfied for our own good?

You don't have to be a genius to see that a nation full of overeating, pill-popping, TV-watching, iPod-wired, shopaholic, attention-deficit-disordered people is not going to make it. We could be headed for extinction if we don't watch out. And if we really *do* aspire to be great again, we've got our work cut out for us.

If this is the price of success, I'd rather lose.

I want to talk about a few of the things I'm experiencing these days that disturb me about our culture. These are more than just pet peeves. In many ways we've lost our compass, and we don't know whether we're coming or going. Leadership isn't just a matter of putting someone at the front of the parade—unless you're a *lemming*. All of us have to develop leadership qualities and nurture them in our children. Qualities such as responsibility, accountability, discipline, and community spirit.

GARBAGE IN, GARBAGE OUT

Sometimes I wonder if we'd be better off with less success. Maybe our minds are getting a little warped. We have five hundred TV channels, plus the Internet. Too much TV, too much Internet, too many e-mails. I'm not knocking computers, but as the saying goes, *garbage in, garbage out.* Do you ever stop and think about how you're actually benefiting from this brave new computer world? I made the mistake of giving my cousin my e-mail address. This guy loves to tell jokes. He sent me fifty-three jokes—all dirty. Who has the time—or the interest?

Our society is the most affluent in the history of mankind. Nobody ever had it so good, and yet all you ever hear about is how depressed everyone is, how anxious, how nervous. What's going on? I'd like to see the statistics for how many other countries in the world are being plagued by similar ills. I wonder how many Japanese and Chinese kids are being treated for ADD/ADHD.

Isn't it time for us to admit that we've become a pill-popping society? We think there's a little blue or white or pink or yellow pill for whatever ails us, and the drug companies are even selling direct to the customer big time. "Ask your doctor if [fill in the blank medication] is right for you." If we're not careful, we're going to medicate ourselves right out of being.

THE ISSUE THAT EATS AT ME

Sometimes the dichotomy of my life gives me the bends. One day I'm trying to do something about fat kids dying in America, and the next day I'm trying to do something about malnourished kids dying someplace else. What's wrong with this picture? People in Darfur are starving to death, and we're eating five thousand calories a day of fast food. Are we nuts?

I told you about my work with Nourish the Children. Most of my energies for the past twenty-two years have gone to my foundation, whose mission it is to find a cure for diabetes. I started the Iacocca Foundation in 1984, after my wife Mary died from complications of type 1 diabetes. Type 1 diabetes is caused by the destruction of the pancreatic islet cells that produce insulin. It is a devastating disease, and can lead to an early death. I made it my mission to find a cure. The Iacocca Foundation is mostly dedicated to medical research. I hope this work becomes my legacy. We're lucky to have some smart, highly motivated people running the foundation—starting with my daughter Kathi, who is the president, and Dana Ball, our executive director. My younger daughter Lia is also involved, as a foundation trustee. We're getting close to a cure, and I still think it may happen in my lifetime. But I'm not counting my white mice before they're hatched because medical research is a one-step-forward, two-steps-back kind of deal.

The world of medical research has been a real education for me. I guess I shouldn't have been surprised to find that it suffers from the same kind of leadership malaise we're seeing in the rest of society. I'm learning that research is a lot like government—kind of a self-generating bureaucracy. You do research so you can write papers to get more funding to do more research to write more papers. This was a big shock to me when I finally figured it out. I said, "Hey, isn't anyone trying to find a *cure*?"

The most innovative research is often killed during the peer review process. Why? Well, let me put it to you simply: Imagine if every time Chrysler wanted to bring a new car to market, it had to depend on positive reviews from GM and Ford. Are you starting to get the picture?

Let me tell you a little story. In 2001, Dr. Denise Faustman, a longtime Iacocca Foundation–supported researcher, approached our board. Dr. Faustman is an associate professor at Harvard Medical School and a researcher at Massachusetts General Hospital. I happen to think she's brilliant *and* dedicated, which is a winning combination. Dr. Faustman told us that she had remarkable data from a project funded by the foundation. It was one of those thrilling "Eureka!" moments of discovery in our work. Dr. Faustman had spent eight years trying to identify the source of the autoimmune attack that causes type 1 diabetes. In the process, she identified the bad cells that are responsible for the disease. After eliminating them in mice with drug therapy, she reported for the first time that regeneration of the damaged adult stem cells was possible. Suddenly, there was light at the end of the tunnel. We believed that human trials were not that far away. In 2003, Dr. Faustman published another paper that confirmed the regeneration project, and that's when the gloves came off.

Suddenly the diabetes research community was up in

arms. Things got ugly. Competing organizations got the word out to donors that Dr. Faustman was a fraud. It was an undignified free-for-all. When we tried to keep discussions focused on science, people acted like angry children, name-calling, and trying to discredit both Dr. Faustman and the Iacocca Foundation. They saw regeneration as a threat, all right. A threat to the *regeneration* of their funding.

It took a while, but the major research organizations eventually came around. Today, even the Juvenile Diabetes Research Foundation admits that regeneration is one of the most promising research directions. But the process was bloody.

The politics of stem cell research is a costly distraction. While everyone is busy fighting about embryonic stem cells, we're missing a big chance to make breakthroughs with adult stem cells. For the past twenty years, adult stem cells have proven their success. We use them to regenerate bone marrow, blood, and skin. Embryonic stem cells, on the other hand, have never cured a single disease or been used in a single therapy. We don't even know if they're capable of it. So, why don't we go with what we know—*regeneration*—instead of wasting our time debating about some distant fantasy of a miracle with embryonic stem cells? Once again, I have to ask, does anyone out there really want a *cure*?

Sometimes the medical research organizations get so busy raising money and running their bureaucracies that they lose sight of the mission. The National Institutes of Health, funded by our tax dollars, spend billions of dollars a year on diabetes. *You* try to find out where the money goes. And if you do, let me know, because *I* sure haven't had any luck getting information.

We've got to remember that we're talking about real people here. Diabetes is a terrible disease that basically kills you
from the inside out. Watching Mary die was a slow, agonizing
process. Nothing could stop the progress of the disease, and the
worst part for me was that overwhelming sense of helplessness.
Mary was only fifty-seven years old when she died and she suffered terribly.

Mary didn't live to see her two gorgeous daughters get
married. She never had a chance to know her seven grandchildren, or to see them growing into the kind of adults she would be
proud of. If I can do something to keep this tragedy from happening to another family, I'm going to give it my all.

A NEW EPIDEMIC

What has been discouraging is that even as we've made progress
in research on type 1 diabetes, there is a growing epidemic of
obesity—especially childhood obesity—which leads to type 2
diabetes, a condition that prevents the insulin-producing cells
from functioning normally. The Centers for Disease Control
and Prevention estimates that one out of every three American
children born in 2000 will develop diabetes in their lifetime.
How do you start fixing *that* problem?

Well, first you have to ask why it exists in the first place.
When you get to the core of the problem you find that it's
behavior-based, which is the toughest challenge of all. Most type
2 diabetes can be attributed to obesity and a sedentary lifestyle,
which cause insulin resistance. More than sixty million Ameri-

cans are obese, and the number is growing, right along with the waistlines.

Some researchers are working on a magic pill so you can eat all the crap you want and not get fat. Others are talking about gastric-bypass surgery as a therapy for type 2 diabetes. In other words, we're still looking for the instant fix. We want to stay fit and trim while stuffing ourselves in front of the TV, instead of exercising and eating right. Listening to people talk about getting their stomachs stapled as a cure for obesity is one of the most depressing things I've ever heard.

The Iacocca Foundation, whose original mission has been to find a cure for type 1 diabetes (insulin-dependent), has now had to spend more money to address type 2 diabetes. It's naïve to think there is a quick fix. We've got to face up to the truth: We created this problem by indulging our desire for instant gratification. Instead of using our heads and our God-given free wills and intellects, we've reverted to our basest natures. I call it the goldfish principle. If you've ever had goldfish, you know what I'm talking about. You have to regulate how much of the fish food you sprinkle in the tank every day. If you pour too much in, the goldfish will keep eating until they literally blow up. They don't have a signal that says stop. It sounds an awful lot like twenty-first-century America.

HOPE TAKES WORK

I'm still learning that there is no such thing as *easy* when it comes to accomplishing big goals. A couple of years ago, when we realized that we'd need $11.5 million to get Dr. Faustman started on a human clinical trial, I said, "No problem. I can raise $11.5 million in a heartbeat. All I need is myself and ten other rich guys." I plunked down my million dollars and started calling my friends. I didn't get too far, although I am thankful for a good friend who anonymously joined me at the $1 million level and to many others who contributed. But I realized that my friends had their own causes. I had to remind myself once again that the important stuff is never easy.

What did I do? I returned to the playbook I used to raise money for the Statue of Liberty–Ellis Island Commission. I went to the people. We started a campaign called Join Lee Now, and asked Americans for small donations. They came pouring in—the average gift is $75—and since the beginning they have contributed more than $2 million.

Then I got *really* creative. I made a deal with Chrysler to film four commercials for $1.5 million, with the money going to the foundation. As part of the deal, Chrysler and its dealers agreed to donate one dollar for every car they sold between November 2005 and December 2006, and they raised $3 million.

The commercials were part of a campaign to woo young buyers to Chrysler. The one that got the most attention paired me with the hip-hop icon Snoop Dogg. It was called "Golfing Buddies," and they put us on a golf course in a souped-up golf cart during the shoot. It was 102 degrees that day and the shoot took almost eight hours.

Snoop Dogg seemed like a nice kid, but I never understood a word he said.

I got a kick out of how Chrysler used my famous pitch line

from the eighties—"If you can find a better car, buy it"—and translated it into Snoop Dogg–speak: "If the ride is more fly, then you must buy." What I'll do for the cause!

I still enjoy a challenge, and I always feel as if I get back more than I give. That's what I'd like to pass on to the younger generation—the rewards of being involved. I've started with my own grandkids. I want them to know how *lucky* they are to be in a position to give back—because they have been *given* so much.

I've been heartened lately to read that young people are getting involved in volunteering again. The "9/11 generation" experienced a jolt of reality, and their response has been to reach out. Applications for the Peace Corps are at record levels. I hope the trend continues. Who wouldn't want to live in a country whose leaders have altruistic, charitable hearts? In the race to determine who will own the twenty-first century, I'll place my bets on the givers, not the takers.

XVIII

Bring back brain power

You know you're in trouble when the President of the United States asks, "Is our children learning?" But it isn't just the intellectually challenged who are missing the boat on education. We've all got to get real—and get serious—because our ability to compete and prosper as a nation depends on our children being well educated and prepared to live in this complex world.

Year after year, the statistics show the same thing: American students struggle to hold their own, compared to students in other countries—especially in math and science. The latest international rankings in math and science just came out. Who was at the top?

1. South Korea
2. Japan
3. Singapore

Where was the United States? Number eighteen of twenty-four. That's just plain shameful.

A lot of you may not remember the last time we fell behind in math and science. It was 1957, and that year the Soviet Union (our archenemy in the cold war) launched Sputnik, the first man-made satellite, into space. Americans just went crazy. We couldn't let that stand. The government began pouring money into math and science education. Twelve years later, we put the first man on the moon.

I believe that most parents care about the quality of their kids' schools. But too often they're blind to what's really going on. They don't know how to evaluate quality. In a recent Gallup poll, 76 percent of parents said they were satisfied with their children's schools. A lot of them pointed to the fact that their kids were getting good grades. But what they have to understand is that just because a kid is doing well against his peers in America, doesn't mean he's doing *well*. We're not getting clobbered by Japan, South Korea, and Singapore in math and science scores because their kids are smart and disciplined and ours are stupid and lazy. They're clobbering us because their parents and their schools demand more of them. In America our kids attend school 180 days a year. Japanese kids go to school 240 days a year. If we want our kids to catch up, you'd think we'd at least start by sending them to school for as long as the kids in Japan. The three-month summer vacation is a sacred cow. I once wrote a newspaper column calling for the extension of the school year. I got bombarded for *that* lousy idea—mostly from teachers. One of them even made her class write to the mean old Grinch who wanted to steal their summer vacation. Do you know how it feels to get twenty-eight pieces of mail from nine-year-olds, telling you in big block letters that you're a dope?

The truth is, I'm not fully convinced that more school days equals quality education. The real key is how you introduce kids to the basics. I've always believed that the ten-year span from five to fifteen is the make-or-break time. That's when the fundamentals have to be instilled. And the people we charge with this priceless task are our schoolteachers.

NO TEACHER LEFT BEHIND?

The prestige of classroom teaching in this country is pretty low. How do I know? Because while we pay lip service to how important teachers are, we don't do anything tangible to support our words. If this were a company, and teachers were valued employees, what would the company do? It would recruit them aggressively. It would invest in training. It would compensate them well. It would provide ways for them to share their expertise. It would take note of those who really excel. We do none of those things with teachers. And how many parents are encouraging their kids to become teachers? "Are you crazy?," they say. "Nobody can live on a teacher's salary."

We're really upside down. In a completely rational society, teachers would be at the tip of the pyramid, not near the bottom. In that society, the best of us would aspire to be teachers, and the rest of us would have to settle for something less. The job of passing civilization along from one generation to the next ought to be the highest honor anyone could have.

Too bad we don't live in that perfect world. Judging by pay and prestige, teaching school ranks pretty close to the bottom of all professions requiring a college education. The average starting salary for new teachers is about 30 percent less than the average starting salary for all other college graduates. How can the teaching profession attract the best and brightest when there's so little incentive?

Even our President brags about having been a C student. He ran against Al Gore and John Kerry, two extremely well-educated men, and mocked their "fancy, elite" educations. It was a bit disingenuous, since Bush attended Yale and Harvard. But he loves to play the "average" card. Bush was the cool kid who never studied, and he ran on that platform.

He also ran on the No Child Left Behind program, which he proclaimed as his proudest achievement while governor of Texas. Only after Bush managed to push the program through Congress as a federal mandate did we learn that the Texas record was not exactly sterling. An inquiry into the Texas No Child Left Behind program revealed widespread test-rigging and numbers-fudging by educators and administrators. I guess they were thinking that desperate times required desperate measures. And that's the problem with No Child Left Behind. It promotes desperation. That's what you get when you set up a rigid formula for judging excellence that is entirely test-based and doesn't account for the thousands of variables that constitute learning. Oh, and by the way, it would help if the government would fully *fund* the mandate before it saddled struggling school districts across the country with the burden.

LET'S GET BACK TO BASICS

Too many teachers start out dedicated to this noblest of professions and wind up selling real estate or becoming computer programmers by their mid-thirties because they're burned out, or disillusioned, or need more money, or are just plain tired of being at the bottom of the pyramid.

Looking back, I have to wonder what happened. I remember the great teachers I had as a kid. Everyone in town looked up to them, not just the kids. There were a few of them who had more influence on my life than anybody else outside my own family.

It wasn't *that* long ago, but you've got to admit that if I still remember individual teachers, they must have really been something. When I was in the ninth grade, I had a teacher named Miss Marian Raber. She's memorable because she taught me to communicate in writing. That lesson in organizing my thoughts and presenting my ideas cogently has been of lasting value.

Maybe the problem today is that teachers don't have time for the basics because they're too busy being cops and social workers and surrogate parents and drug counselors and psychiatrists. As if being a teacher weren't hard enough!

Teachers today have a brand-new problem to worry about—getting *shot* in the classroom. As I write this, I'm looking at three school shootings just in the last week—even though most schools have metal detectors.

I think maybe a little tough love is in order—and a lot of people are going to scream, but hear me out. Why don't we say that every kid has a right to go to school in this country—until the first time he shows up with a gun, a switchblade, or a little white bag of coke. Then we write him off. Send him packing. Think of it as a form of educational triage.

Here's the way I see it. There are some kids who will make it no matter what you do or don't do. Then, there's the large majority who need a lot of help to make it. And finally, there are some who just can't be helped, and who suck up all of the resources and attention like a black hole.

While I'm at it, here's another idea that will have people up in arms. Let's learn the value of failure. The word *flunk* isn't even in the vocabulary of our schools anymore. At some point all the childhood development experts and psychologists got together and said it was emotionally damaging to tell a kid he'd failed. Their motto: "No child left behind, even if he can't read!"

There's a word for that in my book. It's called malpractice. I think a teacher who passes a student who can't do the work is no different than a surgeon who sews you up with a sponge still inside. Kids can handle flunking the fifth grade. The real killer is *not* flunking and finding out ten years down the road that they don't have the basic skills to earn a living.

Maybe those experts could use a lesson from General George Patton, who said, "I don't measure a man's success by how high he climbs but by how high he bounces when he hits bottom."

Our high school dropout rate is a tragedy. But an even bigger tragedy is the number of high school graduates who can barely read their diplomas. (I've got to confess that I couldn't read *my* diploma, either. But mine was written in Latin.)

These kids will find themselves competing with high school graduates overseas who *can* read their diplomas—some even in Latin, or any one of four or five different languages. And that's the bottom line: the ability to compete. Let's not cheat our children and our nation out of that.

LEARNING BY READING

I can't leave this subject without making a pitch for reading. Since you're reading this, I want to thank you for buying my book. If you borrowed it from the library, don't forget to return it. I hope you learn a little bit, and maybe crack a smile every few pages. But even if you weren't reading my book, it would be fine with me—as long as you're reading *something*.

A word to parents: The biggest favor you can do for your kids is to have plenty of books around the house. Read *to* them, read *around* them, be a family that reads. (And if you're not such a good reader yourself, it's never too late to learn.)

Show me a kid who loves to read—I don't care if it's a comic book, a science fiction novel, or a book about the history of dinosaurs—and I'll show you a kid who's going to do well in life. My parents weren't highly educated people. Pop made it through the fourth grade, and Mom through the third grade. But in our household, my sister and I were encouraged to read. I was voracious, and I could be a bit of a show-off with my newfound knowledge. I remember a day in the third grade when we were studying the Greeks, and our teacher asked if anyone knew the name of Ulysses' dog. My hand shot up. For some reason I knew the answer, and I won the admiration of my teacher and the other kids—at least for that day.

I especially loved vocabulary. I got a kick out of words. I still do. I'm always looking for the best word to describe my thoughts. That's why I went through about twenty drafts to write this book. I drove everyone crazy.

The idea of writing a book never occurred to me until I was sixty years old. But once it took hold, I realized that a lifetime of reading had taught me how to form a coherent thought and tell a story and speak my mind on the page. Reading and writing are still my favorite pastimes. Oh, and I like to talk, too.

XIX

Three men
who taught me to lead

Since nobody is born a leader, you need someone to teach you how to walk and talk and *be* one. You need a mentor. I was lucky enough to have three: Nicola Iacocca, Charlie Beacham, and Robert McNamara. They were my mentors. And sometimes they were my *tor*-mentors. Let me tell you what they taught me.

NICOLA IACOCCA: OPTIMISM

You couldn't grow up the son of a man like Nicola Iacocca and not want to emulate him. My father was not an educated man, but he had an inner confidence that just blew you away.

I've written about my father before because he was my number one mentor in life. I can't imagine who I would have been without his influence.

To this day, it's hard for me to fathom how he managed—all by himself—to travel to America at the age of twelve. He came to live with his half brother in Garrett, Pennsylvania, and the first thing they did was put him to work in the mines. I guess there were a lot of stories like that—young kids sent here to become what amounted to slave laborers. But even that young, my father had a special spark of self-knowledge. He worked for one day in the mine, and he said to himself, "I left the farm and the open air of Italy for *this*?" So he ran away to Allentown, Pennsylvania, where another brother lived. He always said that his one day in the mines was the only day he spent working for somebody else.

My father was an unbelievable guy for someone who'd just been through the fourth grade. But I think he was a classic example of the way God gives some people more common sense and street smarts than others. He was gifted—a natural-born entrepreneur. He was always resourceful. By the time he was thirty-one he'd saved enough money to return to Italy to bring over his widowed mother. While he was there he fell in love with my mother, the seventeen-year-old daughter of a shoemaker, and he brought her back, too.

The voyage to America was hard on his young wife. She contracted typhoid fever on the ship. That could have been the end for my mother. Normally they were pretty strict about not letting sick people into the country. Ellis Island would have been her last stop. But somehow she made it past the inspectors. In later years I asked, "Pop, how did you get Mom through Ellis Island?" He never answered directly, just gave me a great big smile and said something like this: "I'd been here a long time. I knew this business. You do what you have to do." In other words, he paid somebody off. I guess you'd call it minor corruption, but my father never regretted it for a minute, and I have to say that I didn't, either. Who knows where I'd be if they'd rejected Mom. As it was, I had the luck of the draw. I was born in the U.S.A. three years after she arrived.

Soon after that my father opened a hot-dog restaurant called the Orpheum Wiener House. Pop believed the food business was a hedge against poverty because, as he always told me, "People have got to eat." Also, there was no capital investment. He said, "You get a little grill, a little steam heater to heat the buns, and you're ready to go." He made a special chili sauce that he'd copied from a vendor on Coney Island. Later he brought my uncles over to help run the business. They were the hot-dog kings of Allentown, and they still are. Today the restaurant is run by their sons and grandsons. It's called Yocco's, which is pretty much how the Pennsylvania Dutch pronounce *Iacocca*. The family made a good living on the nickel hot dog. It's a *dollar* hot dog now, of course.

My father couldn't sit still for just one business. He had so many interests. He was nuts about cars, and he owned one of the first Model Ts. Even when I was a little kid, I can remember he had some cars that worked and some that didn't. He bought into a fledgling national rental company called U-Drive-It, and at one point, he had a fleet of about thirty Model Ts. I'm sure that I inherited my love of cars from my father.

My father's never-say-die energy and optimism left an imprint on me. You couldn't watch him and *not* think the sky was the limit. Even during the Depression he got by. He always found a way. Maybe it's because he never had time for self-doubt. The world was a big canvas, he always said. If an endeavor or a relationship didn't work out, there was always something else to try and someone else to meet.

He was open to life. He'd say, "You've got to have adversity. Otherwise, how will you know the difference when things are good?" I didn't inherit that gene. I was a worrier. Optimism wasn't a natural state for me. When I was worried about something, he'd prod me. "*Lido*, you've got to roll with the punches more. Do you remember what was on your mind a year ago?" And I'd say, "How could I remember? A lot of things happen in a year." He'd pull out some notes with a flourish, and say, "I have it written down." Then he'd proceed to tell me about something that had made me unhappy a year ago, and deliver the punch line: "You can't even remember it now." He understood life's ebbs and flows, and that core of optimism made him unstoppable.

My father also had the quality that these days they call self-esteem. I never saw him hang back or think he wasn't good enough to talk to anyone. I wish I could emulate him and be more easygoing. He was completely relaxed in every situation. Henry Ford II himself enjoyed my dad. He'd sometimes come over to the house—and he hardly ever did that because he was against fraternizing with the employees. I remember how he'd arrive with Christina, his beautiful Italian wife. We'd have a big Italian meal. My mother did the cooking, and my father did the talking. He and Ford got along. I remember Ford saying to Pop, "I don't know how I could run this company without your son." (Later on, I guess he figured out a way.)

Of course, my father had great expectations for his only son, and the other side of his warmth and benevolence was that he was a big disciplinarian. Maybe too much of a disciplinarian by today's standards. Verbally he could assault me and hurt me, but he never touched me.

Sometimes he was just too hard to please. When I graduated from high school, I was number twelve in a class of more than eight hundred. I was proud of myself. I said to Pop, "Not bad, huh?"

Pop said, "Why weren't you first?" It was his way of saying "never be satisfied."

But what made the biggest impression on me was Pop's optimism. No matter how bad things got, he always found the silver lining. I never knew the meaning of the word *impossible*. It wasn't spoken in our home.

CHARLIE BEACHAM: COMMON SENSE

Charlie Beacham really broke the mold. If I learned from my father that you didn't need a fancy education to be wise, I learned from Charlie Beacham that you could have a fancy education and still be street-smart.

Charlie Beacham was my first business mentor. I loved the guy—and I have to say I'd never met anyone like him. He was a big, warm, tough-talking Southerner who had such a talent for being a "regular guy" that it was a surprise to find he had a master's in engineering from Georgia Tech.

His expansive personality and love of people convinced

Charlie to shift his ambition from engineering to sales and marketing. He was the Eastern regional manager of Ford when I got a job as zone manager in Wilkes-Barre, Pennsylvania.

I was as green as grass. Charlie used to say about me and all the other newbies, "You boys are so green I'm worried when I send you out in the field the cows'll eat you up."

Charlie understood that book learning only got you so far. One of the first things he did was send me to a Ford truck center to work the showroom for three months. I wasn't happy. I said, "I went to college. I got a master's degree. What am I doing selling used trucks in the middle of nowhere?" And Charlie said, "Because that's where the business is—on the showroom floor. To hell with all your book learning. You've gotta go figure out what happens when a guy comes in who's willing to pay you thousands of dollars for a car or truck."

Charlie impressed on me that in the car business there were no direct sales. Everything was sold through a network of independent dealers. Selling cars was all about the dealers. It was a lesson I never forgot.

In Charlie's common-sense world people strove to be great, but everyone made mistakes along the way. That was part of the learning process, too. I remember once I was down in the dumps because my district had come in last in sales. Charlie saw me walking through the garage, slumped with defeat, and he came over and put a big arm around me. "What are you so down about?" he asked.

"Well," I said dejectedly, "there are thirteen zones and mine was thirteenth in sales this month."

"Aw, hell," he said. "Don't let *that* get you down. *Some-*

body's got to be last." Then he gave me a sharp look. "But listen," he added, "just don't be last two months in a row."

Charlie had that rare quality in a boss—the ability to motivate you even when you were struggling. He wasn't like the boss who jumps on every mistake and rules by intimidation. The one thing he couldn't stand was people who wouldn't admit they'd screwed up. He used to grumble, "Everybody makes mistakes. The trouble is that most people won't own up to them. They'll try to put the blame on their wife, their mistress, their kids, the dog, the weather—anything but themselves. So if you screw up, don't give me any excuses. Go look in the mirror, and then come to me."

Charlie always encouraged me. If an idea was good—that is, if it passed the common-sense test—he was all for it. And that's how I got my big break. In 1956 we were in the middle of a slump. Sales of the new Fords were lousy everywhere, but they were *really* lousy in Pennsylvania. So I came up with a plan: Any customer could buy a 1956 Ford for a 20 percent down payment, followed by three years of monthly payments of $56. I called it "56 for 56." At the time, financing the purchase of cars for more than a year was a new idea, and our sales really took off. Within three months, the Philadelphia district went from last in sales to first. Charlie was so proud of me that he wrote a personal note to Robert McNamara, the vice president of the Ford Division. (Charlie always said, "If you want to give a man *credit*, put it in writing. If you want to give him *hell*, do it on the phone.") McNamara adopted "56 for 56" as a national program, and the program was responsible for selling an extra 75,000 cars. I was promoted to district manager of Washington, D.C., and my future suddenly seemed a whole lot brighter.

Another thing that made it brighter was love. I'd met Mary McCleary when she was a receptionist at the Ford plant in Chester. She was a beauty—with auburn hair, green eyes, and a sparkling personality. We were planning to get married and we had purchased a house in Washington, D.C. Once again, I was the luckiest guy in the world. Then Charlie called me. He'd been promoted to car and truck sales manager for the Ford Division, and he wanted to bring me to Dearborn as his national truck marketing manager.

"You've gotta be kidding," I sputtered. "I'm getting married next week and I just bought a house."

He chuckled, and then said gruffly, "I'm sorry, but if you want to get paid, your paycheck will be in Dearborn." I may have protested, but I think Charlie knew how thrilled I was.

Charlie was my angel. He made things happen for me. He loved me, and he sold me to McNamara. I realize now that the smartest move of my career was to follow the leader—Charlie Beacham—to Detroit.

ROBERT MCNAMARA: DISCIPLINE

When Robert McNamara's name comes up, most people say, "Oh, yeah, wasn't he the guy who got us into Vietnam?" It's a tough legacy, but it's only part of the story. Robert McNamara had a life before JFK picked him to be secretary of defense, and that life was at Ford Motor Company.

McNamara joined Ford the same year I did—in 1946. The difference was that I was just a student engineer and he'd already made a name for himself. He was one of a group of army officers in World War II known as the "Whiz Kids." He was a statistical genius who helped plan weapons strategy. McNamara had that rare gift for analyzing a situation and set-ting the right course—which was just what Ford needed after the war. Henry Ford II had just come on board to run his grand-father's company, which was hobbling along and losing money. He brought in the Whiz Kids to help him do it.

McNamara quickly became one of Henry Ford's key go-to guys. He was also kind of an odd duck in the Ford culture. He and his wife didn't live in Bloomfield Hills or Grosse Point like the other execs. They lived in Ann Arbor, near the University of Michigan. Bob had the mentality of a professor and the soul of a liberal. And he was way ahead of his time. He was pushing for small cars, safety features, and the environment back in the fifties, if you can imagine that. He used to say that business lead-ers had a duty to serve society as well as their shareholders, and that a company could drive for profits and at the same time meet social responsibilities. He was guided by this principle: "There is no contradiction between a soft heart and a hard head."

My first impression of Bob McNamara was pretty much like everyone else's—the guy lacked a certain *warmth*. He was so focused that he didn't always have time for niceties—and he hated golf. He once said, "It's crazy. You don't use your mind on a golf course. You take this little white ball and you try to put it in a little hole a couple hundred yards away, and you spend your whole life doing that. What's the point?" It didn't make sense to his logical mind.

I got along with McNamara, though. First of all, he loved

Beacham and Beacham loved me. So I was in. But we also developed a strong relationship because I learned so much from him, and I took those lessons to heart.

Bob was a visionary, but there was no pie in the sky where he was concerned. He was the original "show me where it's working" guy. Bob never let me get out of the room with an idea that hadn't been analyzed a hundred different ways. He used to tell me, "Lee, you're so effective one on one. You could sell anyone anything. But we're about to spend one hundred million dollars here. Go home tonight and put your great idea on paper. If you can't do that, then you haven't really thought it out. Don't sell me with the force of your personality. Sell me with the facts."

It was one of the most important lessons I ever learned. From that time on, whenever one of my people had an idea, I'd tell him to put it in writing.

Bob became a great ally of mine, and he taught me discipline. You have to have a vision, but it's got to be grounded in reality. *Put it in writing. Put it in writing.* To this day it's my motto.

Bob had just become president of Ford when JFK tapped him for the job of secretary of defense. You can't help but wonder about the kind of company Ford might have become if McNamara had been at the helm for a decade or so. If he'd lasted that long. I didn't appreciate until after Bob had gone just how difficult it was to work for Henry Ford II. Ford liked to attract the best and the brightest. The problem was, he couldn't stand to have strong leaders around who might outshine him. It increased my admiration for Bob knowing how smoothly he'd skated over the treacherous surface of Ford's executive office.

A SPECIAL THANKS TO THE WOMEN

I started my career in an era when there were no women leaders in the car business. If you ask me, it's still behind the times in that respect. We like to romanticize the "car guy," but are resistant to the idea that maybe we need a few more "car *gals.*"

My mentors in business were all male, but there were two women who became my mentors in *life* — my mother and my wife Mary.

My mother taught me LOVE. And the way she did that was by *showing* love every day of her life.

We were always close, but we grew even closer when I got older, especially after Pop died. I really enjoyed my mom. When she was in her seventies, she could still run circles around me. I loved taking her along to business conventions and on vacations. There was almost no one I'd rather spend an evening with than Mom, and I talked to her on the phone just about every day.

Like everyone else in the Iacocca family, Mom always spoke her mind. She did her best to keep me on the straight and narrow. She thought I worked too hard. She disapproved when I got a divorce from my second wife. She made virtue sound like common sense. Her moral code was from a simpler time — but we could sure use more of it today.

They say that when a parent dies — even when the parent is ninety and you're seventy — you feel like an orphan. I can attest to that. When Mom died in 1994 at the age of ninety, I was bereft. I think she knew me better than anyone — not the public persona, but the real me. It's good to have someone around who knows the real you.

The other woman who taught me about life was, of course, my wife Mary. I'd have to say that Mary's greatest gift to me was a lesson in COURAGE. Mary had a fiery spirit. *Nothing* daunted her. In fact, it almost seemed like she was energized by adversity. Mary wasn't a hand-wringer. She was a *doer*.

Even in the final years, when life was so hard for her, she'd just shrug and say, "You think *I* have it bad. You should see the *other* patients." Mary never spent a moment complaining, and her thoughts in the final days were of me and the girls. "I'm so proud of you," she said to me a couple of weeks before she died. I wish I'd had the presence of mind to say how proud I was of *her*.

I hope when my time comes I can face death with even a little bit of the same courage Mary showed. She was a shining light until the end.

HAVE A MENTOR, BE A MENTOR

So, I was the luckiest guy in the world. I had three devoted mentors to teach me optimism, common sense, and discipline. I had wonderful, strong women to teach me love and courage. I've tried to return the favor by being a mentor to others. I want to challenge everyone now—whether you're a parent, an educator, an executive, an uncle or aunt—to find that lesson of lasting value that you can pass along. And if you're a young person getting started today, the first thing you need to do, before you even find your desk in a new company, is to find the person who is going to be your teacher and advocate.

I admire leaders who take time out to be mentors. One example is New York Yankees owner George Steinbrenner. I know that people think George is just a bombastic, volatile guy, but he's been my friend for many years, and as far as I'm concerned, he's a big softie. George doesn't wear his good deeds on his sleeve, but in his lifetime he has helped many young athletes achieve their dreams. He has dedicated himself to supporting kids who have the talent and drive to succeed. I'll bet that legacy will have more long-term impact than his team's World Series titles.

When I was thinking about how important mentors are, I realized that kids have to be guided to seek out the right mentors. In the Catholic Church, every newborn baby has a godfather (no, not *that* kind) and a godmother who promise to guide the child's moral and spiritual development. When I was a kid, godparents took their role seriously. I think we've lost some of that dedication in raising our kids.

Parents have to provide some direction for their children about the people they emulate. You have to talk openly with them about the people they admire. Who are their heroes? Why do they want to emulate a particular person? We're a celebrity-driven culture, so chances are your kids admire sports and entertainment personalities. Push them to defend their heroes. What qualities—apart from the shallow values of money, fame, and good looks—make them worthy of emulation? Ask them to name real people they actually know—teachers, merchants, coaches, pastors, neighbors—who they look up to. Keep having this conversation every chance you get. Your children may roll their eyes, but trust me, they're listening and thinking about it. It's a start.

Remember, leaders aren't born, they're made. It's up to all of us to work at making good leaders. I, for one, can't sit by and ask, "Where have all the leaders gone?" if I'm not ready to look to myself and say, "What have I done lately to mold a young mind?"

XX

Get off the golf course and DO something

I flunked retirement. If there was a handbook of the Dos and Don'ts of retiring, my picture would be on the front cover of the Don't section. In the space of a couple years, I retired, remarried, and moved to a new planet called L.A. I pulled up my roots, said goodbye to my friends, and left behind the world I'd known for almost fifty years. Was I nuts? Well, I must have been temporarily insane to think it was a good idea.

Los Angeles was foreign to me. I didn't speak the language or understand the customs. My friends in Detroit were all in the car business. In L.A., everyone was in the movie business. They read *Variety*. I read *Automotive News*. Almost right away I knew I was in trouble. *Holy shit*, I thought. *What the hell have I done?*

I'd saved Chrysler. Now the question was, could I save *myself*?

My retirement fiasco happened more than a decade ago. Since then, I've learned some lessons about what *not* to do. But most important, I figured out what *to* do. It has been a revelation to me that you can be retired and still have a life of meaning. Today, at eighty-two, I'm in good health, I'm active, and I'm engaged in the world around me. I guess that's why so many people in their late fifties and early sixties come to me asking for advice. When they get close to retirement, they start to panic. They wonder what they're going to do with the next twenty or thirty years. Fear grabs them in the gut. For some of them it's the first time they've ever been afraid of *anything*. And what is the fear? That their lives will stop mattering.

I know the feeling. Work is like oxygen. Even if you have a family you love, and hobbies you enjoy, and you go to church or synagogue every week, there is nothing that replaces work. Your work holds it all together. Don't let anyone tell you differently.

When you're a CEO, it's even more intoxicating—and somewhat unreal. You never wash a car, you never fill a gas tank, you never pick up a tab. When you travel, there's always an entourage leading you around. You go to the finest restaurants. You stay in the presidential suite. People wait on you hand and foot. You live in a bubble. You go all over the world, but you don't see much beyond the airport, the hotel lobby, and the convention center. You may be at the hub of your little universe, but you're isolated. Then you retire, and you don't know how to be an average Joe.

A lot of people would just as soon *not* retire. They'd like to keep doing what they're doing until the boys in the white coats carry them out of the corner office. But you've got to be realistic. There isn't a business in the world that can't use an infusion of fresh blood at some point. And the only way that happens is for the old blood to move out.

Someone once said they had to force me to retire from Chrysler. Not true. I was turning sixty-eight, and I *wanted* to retire. I didn't have to. I was on top of the world. I could have stayed around forever. But I felt like I'd done everything. I was getting impatient. The young guys came in to see me, and they were all full of piss and vinegar. Everything was new to them. I couldn't help feeling impatient, and a little bored. I'd listen to their great plans, and I'd be thinking, *Yeah, we tried that about twenty times and it didn't work.* But I didn't want to just sit around sounding like a grumpy old man.

I was lucky. I probably could have done just about anything I wanted. I had plenty of offers. Tex Colbert, who'd been the chairman of Chrysler in the early sixties, asked me how I'd like to be president of Harvard. I don't know how serious he was, but I never explored it. Yankees owner George Steinbrenner, who was an old friend, was on the selection committee for a new baseball commissioner, and he asked me if I'd be interested in that. Looking back, I think maybe I should have considered that one, but at the time it didn't appeal to me.

I almost got into politics. In 1991, Pennsylvania senator John Heinz died in a plane crash. My friend John Murtha came to me with a proposition: Robert Casey, the Democratic governor of Pennsylvania, wanted to appoint me to complete Heinz's term, and then I'd have to run on my own in the fall. Murtha would see to it that I got some juicy committee assignments, and he thought it would be a stepping stone to the presidency for me.

They sent in a brash young guy named James Carville to explain things to me. Carville was blunt and fast-talking. Didn't even stop to ask me what *I* thought about the issues. He shoved some papers at me. "Here is your position on abortion," he said. "Here is your position on jobs. Here is your position on—"

Finally, I interrupted. "Wait just a minute," I said. "Don't I get to—"

"No, no," he dismissed me, "we've already done all the studies and focus groups."

"So, you want me in office, but you'll tell me what to believe?" I asked.

Carville shrugged, and started to continue his lecture. At which point I told him where he could shove it. That was my short-lived flirtation with the U.S. Senate. Senator Iacocca was not to be.

What I *did* decide to do after retirement was work as a consultant for Chrysler for another two years. At the time, I thought it was a pretty good plan. I was relieved to have at least that. The point is, you've got to do *something*.

IS THE GRASS GREENER ON THE GOLF COURSE?

I talk to guys who have worked sixty to eighty hours a week for fifty years, and I ask them, "What are you going to do when you retire?" They say, "I think I'll have some fun. I always dreamed of being able to play golf every day."

Well, I'll tell you what. Anybody who says that is a nut— because it'll bore you in a hurry. It's okay when you're working hard and you take in a round of golf on a Wednesday afternoon, like all the doctors. But if you think you can spend twenty years doing nothing but putting a little white ball in a hole three hundred yards away, you're in for a shock.

Luckily, I never got bit by the golf bug, although it wasn't for lack of opportunity. Henry Ford II decided he wanted to learn golf, and he had access to the greats. When I was a young executive he set me up with the best teachers money could buy. It was kind of amazing, considering I was just an amateur. For a while my instructor was George Fazio, who'd tied Ben Hogan in the U.S. Open before he lost in a sudden-death playoff. I was also coached by Claude Harmon, another great player and teacher. All of this high-level training perfected my golf swing. I guess I was the most overtrained amateur in the world.

The problem was I didn't play much. In the auto business there was never time for a lot of golf. I traveled constantly, and weekends were for my family. If I played golf on a Saturday, the whole day was shot. You were on the course for a few hours, then you had to have a drink with the boys, and if you got a hole in one, you'd have to celebrate forever, and before you knew it, your family time was shot. That wasn't for me. I once got some lessons from Arnold Palmer himself. He told me, "You're pretty good, Lee, but you've got to *play*."

But there was just never time. So all that great training went nowhere. Once I retired, I could have spent more time on the golf course, but as I said, the bug never bit me.

There's nothing wrong with playing golf, but if you think golf is going to be enough to fill your life in retirement, you're mistaken. Even if you love golf, it's not going to get you up in the morning the way work did. You've got to find something *real* to do.

I wish we'd invent another word to describe the period of life after they give you the gold watch. Retirement means "retreat, withdrawal." Actually, retirement isn't the end. It can be a beginning. But you've got to approach it the right way.

NOW WHAT DO I DO?

My retirement party was held in Las Vegas in November 1992. It was *some* party. There were eleven thousand people there, including some big Las Vegas stars. Frank Sinatra was there to sing a farewell, and, unbeknownst to me, the songwriter Sammy Cahn had written special lyrics to "My Way," just for the occasion. Too bad Frank had started celebrating early. He totally missed the lyric on the teleprompter. It was still a thrill for me, though. Frank and I had become pretty good friends over the years. My retirement party was his last public performance.

After I retired, my consulting work kept me traveling back and forth between Detroit and Los Angeles, which wasn't the best thing for my marriage. I finally agreed to move to California full-time. I was so dumb I thought I could save my marriage by buying a big house in a fancy section of L.A. It didn't work that way. We moved into the house in January 1994, but a house can't buy happiness. Our marriage was over by the fall. So there I was, retired, alone, and living in a big house in a strange city. I'd pulled up all my roots in Detroit. You know, when you live in a town for fifty years, and you raise a family there, you have a whole infrastructure—doctors, lawyers, pastors, friends, neighbors. They were all gone. I was a stranger in la-la land. And that's when I started to realize I'd made a big mistake. I should have eased into retirement, not changed everything overnight. You've got to have time to adapt to the new reality, and I hadn't given myself any time.

I was flailing, and the decisions I made weren't that great. During that time, I got involved with Kerkorian on the Chrysler buyout, which gave me a lot of grief. I tried a few other things that didn't work out. Through friends, I got involved in Koo-Koo-Roo, a chicken-restaurant chain, but I found I didn't really want to spend my time in the chicken business. Then I got involved in developing the first electric bike. I thought that made some sense. I'd always followed the baby boomers. I gave them the Mustang when they were young, then the minivan when they settled down and had families. Now I figured I'd give them something for retirement. But the electric bike didn't catch on. Then I partnered with GM on a neighborhood electric car. I spent six or seven million dollars of GM's money to learn that the country wasn't ready for a fully electric car.

The point is, I was grabbing at things because I didn't have a plan. If you don't have a plan, you're going to make mistakes.

HAVE A PLAN

So that was the big lesson. Have a plan for retirement. Obviously, the first thing you have to figure out is the financial aspect. How much do you need for your retirement? Maybe your kids are still in school. Or maybe your kids are from what they call the "boomerang" generation, and they've come back to live with you after college. And if your parents are living, it may be a blessing, but it can also be an expense for their care. So you have to add up the numbers. And maybe it becomes obvious that you have to work full- or part-time because you need the extra income. But even if you're financially secure, you've got to DO something. You've got all this knowledge and experience. You've probably got a heck of a lot of energy if you're in your sixties. If you retire early as part of a buyout, you're *really* not ready for the rocking chair on the front porch. So, what are you going to do?

Maybe you've been so busy working that you missed out on some interest or passion that you'd like to give a whirl to. Maybe you have a business idea that's been rattling around in your head. There's a life out there. You can become a mental case if you don't have some kind of plan.

Getting back to the meaning of retirement, I like to look at life as having three stages. The first is learning. The second is earning. And the third is returning. A lot of the baby boomers are still *yearning* in the third stage, because they're never satisfied. But if you think of retirement as a time of returning—of giving something back to society—it can transform your life.

GIVE SOMETHING BACK

A few years ago, I was having lunch with Warren Buffett in Las Vegas at Steve Wynn's Shadow Creek Golf Club. We were eating cheeseburgers, and Warren was drinking his usual cherry Coke.

Buffett had made a ton of money. He was the second-richest guy in the world, after Bill Gates, worth around $44 billion. And I said to him, "Warren, I read in *Fortune* magazine that you said you were leaving nothing to your heirs. *Zero*. Is that true?"

"Well, not exactly," he said. "I take care of education and health. I give each of them a house and a car—and they're comfortable. But they have to make it on their own."

I was interested. "Yeah, I'm struggling with that same issue right now," I said. "I'm talking about a million dollars here and there."

"Well, I'm talking about a *billion* dollars here and there," he replied, and we laughed.

"Look," he said, getting serious. "What do you think it would do for my kids if I gave each of them a billion dollars? They wouldn't have to work anymore or think anymore. It would wreck them."

Well, we all know now what Warren decided to do with his money. He gave $37 billion to the Bill Gates Foundation—the greatest act of charitable giving in U.S. history. And he didn't wait until he was dead.

Warren has his head on straight when it comes to giving back. A lot of guys say, "Well, I deserve this money. It was *my* genius that earned it." Warren doesn't have that kind of arrogance. He once said, "You know, maybe I have talent, but it wouldn't have gotten me very far if I wasn't lucky enough to be born in a place where the stock market gives you huge rewards. So I think society has some claim on that."

That's leadership. To decide that your life isn't just about making a lot of money, but about being part of a bigger picture.

To get serious about returning something to society. I finally stopped flunking retirement when I started pouring more of my energies into the Iacocca Foundation. It became the central challenge of my retirement to find a cure for diabetes.

The Iacocca Institute at my alma mater, Lehigh University, really did start with giving back. When I was a kid, my parents were very set on my going to college, but they didn't have a lot of money. My mother went to work in a silk factory doing piece work on shirts to try to raise the money. In those days, not many people could afford to go to college. I was given a hand up at Lehigh University, thanks to a scholarship. After graduation, I was able to go on to Princeton for an advanced degree in engineering—something I never could have afforded without financial help. (And, by the way, I was lucky enough to be at Princeton during a special time after World War II, when both Albert Einstein and Robert Oppenheimer were located there at the Institute for Advanced Studies. I used to see Einstein almost every morning on my way to class. I'd say, "Good morning, professor," and he'd nod his head. I enjoyed that small daily connection with history.

It made a big impression on me that some anonymous donor had put money on the line to help a kid like me get the best education. The Iacocca Institute is my way of giving back.

What have I learned from twenty-two years of philanthropy? That it's no different from business. To be successful you have to be focused, have a plan, and stick to it with the help of a great team. This means a strong board of trustees, professional staff, and relevant experts as advisors.

You don't have to have deep pockets to return something to

society in your retirement years. You can volunteer. There are so many programs springing up that match people with know-how and experience with those who need it. The best one I ever saw was the Executive Service Corps, started by the former General Dynamics CEO Frank Pace in the 1960s. It's still going strong. They'll take volunteer experts and send them all over the world to teach people how to build roads, start businesses, set up hospitals, and build pipelines.

Most of the philanthropists I know aren't in it for the glory. They're in it because it energizes them. It makes them happy to see their energy and resources really making a difference.

Frank Sinatra was like that. You don't hear a lot about what a generous guy he was because he never advertised it. I got to know Frank over many years, and he was there during the bleakest time of my life, when Chrysler was on the verge of bankruptcy. Frank came to Detroit to help. He said to me, "If you're working for a dollar, I will, too." He did some commercials for us and spent a couple of days visiting plants. He didn't do it for the publicity. He did it because he gave a damn.

I guess it all comes down to happiness. I ask a lot of people these days, including members of my own family, "Are you happy?" And they mumble—they don't want to come right out and say, "Well, yeah! I never had it so good from a financial standpoint."

But happiness goes way beyond that. If there's one thing I've learned it's that money can't buy happiness. Reminds me of my good friend Henny Youngman, who once said, "What good is happiness? You can't buy money with it." Maybe some people don't realize that's a joke. You've got to feel sorry for them.

I have a pretty good life. I'm busy. I get a lot of joy out of my family. I'm in good health. I hope to live to be one hundred. I think I have a shot at it.

Bob Hope used to come to my house often in his final years. He told me, "You want to live to be one hundred? Here's what you do. Get a massage every day. Start every day with fruit. And have sex every day."

I said, "Let me get this straight. Massage, fruit, sex. Hey, Bob, two out of three ain't bad."

Bob was just over one hundred when he died. I did a short eulogy at his funeral. I was sandwiched between Sid Caesar and Red Buttons. When my name was called, after Sid had given his remarks, Red leaned over and said, "You know my schtick better than I do. Try not to steal all my good jokes."

MY RETIREMENT RULES IN A NUTSHELL

To sum up, here's the best advice I can give anyone who wants to ace retirement:

Count your blessings

Stop to think about how lucky you are to have been born in this era, in this great country. If you've made it to retirement, you're in a good place. You won the lottery just by being born in the U.S.A. If you're *really* lucky, you have your health and are surrounded by family and friends.

Don't disengage from life

A lot of people think that after all the stress of their working lives, they shouldn't have *any* stress when they retire. But there's a word for a stress-free state, and it isn't retirement. It's *death*. Study after study shows that complete retirement means an early trip to the grave. I used to watch the guys at Ford and Chrysler. They'd get their gold watches, and go off into the sunset—and they'd be dead in five years. Don't underestimate the importance of being productive.

My father never retired. He didn't know the meaning of retirement. As he got older, he kept looking for new things to do. Back in 1930 he'd gotten a real estate broker's license, but he never practiced and he lost it. So later in life he decided to pick it up again. He took the broker's exam and flunked it three times before he finally made it. He was pretty proud of that license. And he put it to good use. My multitalented father was a whiz at real estate. That's no surprise. It's a people business, and Pop was all about people.

The secret to good heath is mental challenge, physical activity, engaging with people, and having a purpose. I try to do all those things. I read constantly, and never feel as if I've stopped learning. I walk two miles a day. I watch what I eat.

My only real vice—as you can discern from the picture on the cover of this book—is that I love cigars. But I limit myself to one a day. For years I gave up cigars for the forty days of Lent to prove I wasn't addicted. My daughters always suggested I reverse it—smoke like hell during Lent and give up cigars for the rest of the year.

Figure out what will make you happy

Do your homework. Ask everybody around you what makes them happy. Your kids, your spouse, your friends—anyone you can find.

Ask an aging parent, "How do you feel about life today?"

Once you've collected everyone else's opinions, ask yourself the same question. Then take your answer to heart. Here's a clue: It's *not* money.

Malcolm Forbes used to say, "When you die the one with the most toys wins." I knew Malcolm, and let me tell you, the guy really had some phenomenal toys. But he's still *dead.*

My friend Larry Fisher was a rich guy. He owned major real estate in Manhattan. He once told me, "Lee, you keep saying you can't take it with you. Well, you're just not smart enough. I've got it worked out. I sent $100 million ahead in traveler's checks!"

Hang around with young people

Nothing makes me happier than spending time with my grandchildren. It's fun to be with young people. It also keeps me focused on the future. The old crowd just wants to talk about the past, and that can be depressing. When I'm with the kids, I'm always asking myself, what is the world I want my grandchildren to inherit, and what can I do to make it happen?

Kids will push you to live a little, and that's not such a bad thing. In our family, birthdays are big deals, and I like to go all-out for my grandkids. Last December, for her eleventh birthday, I took my granddaughter and twenty of her closest friends to Disneyland. They talked me into going on the California Screamer, which is one of the scariest roller coasters in the world. There's a 360-degree loop where you're hanging upside down. At one point, as our car was careening down a vertical track, I wondered what I was doing. Wasn't there an age limit on these rides?

My father had a way with young people. They were always coming to him for advice. Why? Because he listened, he cared, and he had common sense. At his funeral, there were lots of young people. I was always impressed that teenage girls trusted my pop. I've tried to have the same kind of influence on my granddaughters.

Be a mentor. Time and advice are free, and they're more important than anything else you can do for the next generation. I make it a point to talk to my grandchildren every week, and to see them often. You can quietly change a young person's life in a one-hour talk over a sandwich or a walk in the park.

Live the hell out of your life—*now*

When I think of people who know what it means to live boldly, I have to give top honors to my friend Carroll Shelby. Even at eighty-four, after a heart transplant, Shelby has more spark than people half his age.

I met Shelby in the early 1960s, when I was a vice president at Ford. We were trying to attract young people by building performance cars that appealed to the racing world. Shelby, who was the most famous race car driver in the world, came to see me. He was burning up the carpets with enthusiasm, a big handsome Texan. Shelby said, "I need twenty-five thousand dollars to build a car that can beat the Corvette." It was an offer we couldn't refuse. That car was the Cobra. It began Ford's serious involvement in the racing world. In the coming years, we entered every race, and it was a pretty big thrill to win the Indianapolis 500, the Daytona 500, and all the other big races with our Ford V-8 engines.

I guess part of it was image. We spent a *lot* of money on racing. But we'd justify it by saying, "Race on Sunday, sell on Monday."

Then, in 1982, when I was trying to restore Chrysler's image, I called Shelby. I needed performance models. We started with the Charger Shelby and the Omni GLH, which were sold as Dodges. GLH, by the way, stood for "Goes Like Hell." It went from zero to sixty miles an hour in about five seconds.

The last time I sat in a car with Shelby was in 1991. The pre-production Viper was the pace car for the opening lap of the Indianapolis 500. Shelby was in the driver's seat, and there were about three hundred thousand people in the stands, cheering like crazy.

Shelby turned to me with his famous grin. "Lee, it's a beautiful day, huh?"

I was a little nervous. "I hope you know how to do this," I said.

"Don't worry, I've done it before," he assured me. Then he reached into his pocket and pulled out three little pills, which he popped into his mouth.

"What's that?" I asked.

"Oh, just my nitro," he said. "When I'm excited, I get a little angina."

"You're kidding me," I said with alarm. "You're going to be driving two hundred miles an hour, and you're taking *nitroglycerine*?" That's when I started praying.

SAY YOUR PRAYERS

No matter how important you *think* you are, you're just a little blip on the screen of time. With the passage of years, when you see that there's a lot more behind you than there is ahead of you, you start praying a little harder.

I never wore my religion on my sleeve, but I've always had

faith. I grew up a Catholic and I still practice. But I never spent a lot of time wondering what comes next. There was too much to do in the here and now.

Getting older has humbled me some, and I say my prayers a little more fervently these days. I'm also more aware of the spiritual leaders in the world, because we need spiritual leadership so desperately.

I've been privileged to meet three popes in my life. I took my parents to Rome in the early sixties and they renewed their vows in the presence of Pope John XXIII. That was pretty special. We had a family audience with Pope Paul VI. I have a photo with the Pope and Kathi and Lia, which is quite a keepsake.

The papal audience that is still fresh in my mind was the one I had with Pope John Paul II about six months before he died. Pope John Paul was doing well that day. His hands were very steady, not shaking from Parkinson's. He smiled at me and said, "You're the car man from California."

"No," I replied, "I'm the car man from *Detroit*."

He gave me a rosary and held my hand for a while. "Pray for me," he said.

I was a little bit flustered. "Isn't that *your* job?" I asked. "I don't know how good I'll be."

He just smiled. Later, I *did* pray for him, because, although he was a great spiritual leader, he was just a human being like you and me. He knew that.

In the last few years I've become friendly with Oral Roberts, who lives near me in California. Oral is a charming, quiet man. He's very humble, and he has a good sense of humor. He even says that humor has kept him alive. He's eighty-nine now, and a little frail, but that doesn't take away from the force of his presence. He's a true spiritual leader. People come from all over the world to see him. He once gave me a Bible, which he'd marked with a yellow highlighter. "These are the passages that are important," he told me. Talk about cutting to the chase!

For my last birthday, Oral gave me an autographed copy of his latest book and this piece of wisdom: "Lee," he said, "everybody's going to die, and they go *someplace*. So just be sure your spiritual bank account has more cash receipts than debt."

There's no escaping mortality, and the older you get the more you're reminded of it. Death is the great equalizer, and we all look pretty much the same lying in the coffin. *Life* is where you can make things happen. So, if when you retire you think, "I'm tired. It's time to relax," think again. As the saying goes, you've got all eternity to catch up on your rest.

2008:
A call to action

In the car business we always said, "Don't forget to ask for the order." So that's what I'm going to do. I'm hoping that now that you've read what I have to say about leadership, you're feeling some passion for the idea that we have to get it right in 2008. Maybe you're pissed off. Maybe you're excited. It doesn't matter, as long as the blood is circulating through your veins and, hopefully, going to your *brain*. We all have to be awake this time around.

Here's my pitch. I'm going to ask you to do something. Actually, I'm going to ask you to do *three* things:

> Give something up
> Put something back in
> Elect a leader

GIVE SOMETHING UP

If you have kids, the two most common words around your household are probably *I want*. Kids are basically selfish creatures. They don't have the maturity to understand that you can't *have* everything you want. That's where the adults come in. The other most common word around your household is probably *No*. Or maybe you say *No, honey*. The point is, once you're an adult, you understand about responsibility. One of my favorite Bible quotations is this one from St. Paul: "When I was a child, I spoke as a child, I understood as a child, I thought as a child; but when I became a man, I put away childish things."

The problem with the way we run elections is that candidates tend to appeal to the child in us, not the adult in us. They try to play Santa Claus. They promise us the moon and the stars.

We've talked about how strange it is that nobody has asked us to sacrifice, even though we're at war. Deep down, we all realize there's something very wrong with this. Unless you actually *know* someone who is serving in Iraq or Afghanistan, it's easy to ignore it altogether. You can get up every day, eat breakfast, brush your teeth, get in your car and drive to work without spending one second of your time thinking about the war.

It shows a bankruptcy of leadership, and it's an insult to our patriotism. But maybe we *deserve* to have our patriotism insulted, because we let it happen.

As adults we know that money doesn't grow on trees, so when your favorite candidate starts telling you he's going to cut your taxes, fund your college education, and give you cheaper prescription drugs, you ought to be thinking, *What's the trade-off? What will I have to give up to get what I want?*

To get in practice for this unusual notion of giving something up, here's an exercise you can do before the election. Make it a game around your dinner table (for those few who still sit around a dinner table).

Pick an issue that's important to you. Let's use health care. Ask yourself what you'd be willing to give up to get health care.

- Would you be willing to give up your mortgage-interest deduction on your income tax?
- Would you be willing to reduce your deduction for dependents?
- Would you be willing to pay five cents more for each gallon of gas?
- Would you be willing to put off having your road paved?

The point is very simple. There's no free lunch. For everything you get, you have to give something back.

PUT SOMETHING BACK IN

Democracy is a two-way street. It's not enough to reap the rewards of living in this wonderful country. Each of us has to put something back in. But when I racked my brain, I couldn't come up with a single recent example of a national leader mentioning that part. The last time a President stood up and made this call it was John F. Kennedy in 1961. At his inaugural address he said, "Ask not what your country can do for you; ask what *you* can do for your country." His words inspired a generation. But it wasn't just the *words*. It was the *action*. In Kennedy's brief presidency, we put the idea of service into practice with noble institutions like the Peace Corps.

You can bet that every presidential candidate in 2008 will have a stump speech that talks about the need for national service of some kind. But let's hold their feet to the fire by demanding details. (I hope the media is listening.) A good idea is still only an *idea* until you put it into action.

We can take it a step further. In our own families, communities, and companies, let's start a dialogue about public service—at the dinner table, in the newspapers, on the blogs, on YouTube—wherever people congregate personally or electronically. When I was a kid, my parents made a point of being involved. My father wrote letters to FDR and Harry Truman. He spoke his mind. He didn't let his lack of formal education stop him. He made sure he had a voice and made a contribution.

ELECT A LEADER

By the time you read this, the 2008 presidential election will be a little more than one year away. And you'll probably already be thinking, *Isn't it over* yet?

I have a question for you: Have you already made up your mind about how you're going to cast your vote? Are you thinking, *I don't care, as long as it's a Democrat* . . . or a Republican . . . *or a member of the Green Party* . . . or a woman . . . *or an African American* . . . or a pro-lifer . . . *or a whatever?*" For the purpose of this discussion, I'd like to ask you to *unmake* up your mind. I know it may be a hard thing to do. But if we're serious about electing a leader, we have to start with evaluating leadership qualities.

LET'S GIVE 'EM THE NINE CS TEST

In the first chapter, I introduced my Nine Cs of Leadership:

CURIOSITY
CREATIVITY
COMMUNICATION
CHARACTER
COURAGE
CONVICTION
CHARISMA
COMPETENCE
COMMON SENSE

These are ideals, and there are very few people — even leaders — who have all of them. But if you look back in history, you'll notice that different times require a different emphasis. Two recent examples make the point. When Jimmy Carter was elected President, people cared more about CHARACTER than CHARISMA. With Ronald Reagan, it was all about CHARISMA and COMMUNICATION.

What are the leadership qualities that *these* times cry out for? I'm going to go out on a limb and name four in 2008: Curiosity, communication, character, and competence.

CURIOSITY: We need an expansive leader who will seek input from a wide range of people, including the contrarians. This leader is interested in mastering a *global* point of view, and strives to understand what motivates people to seek progress around the world.

COMMUNICATION: We need an open leader who doesn't hide the bad news or motivate us with fear. This leader speaks the truth, even when it's hard to hear, and inspires us by asking us to share in the obligations of democracy.

CHARACTER: We need a leader, honed by crisis, who demands equality of sacrifice, starting in the Oval Office.

COMPETENCE: Finally, we need a leader who is committed to making America great again—not just in its ideals but in its factories, farms, communities, and families. We need a problem solver who will assemble the best team to make our nation work.

As you listen to the candidates, keep your checklist in front of you. Ask, Is this a curious, competent communicator? Is this a person of character? Don't settle for less.

JOIN ME

Where have all the leaders gone? They're right here, in this great country. But they need to be called forth.

When I was the chairman of the Statue of Liberty–Ellis

Island Commission, I reached out to Americans, asking them to join me in restoring these symbols of our democracy. And the people responded. When I was passionate about finding a cure for diabetes, I organized a campaign called Join Lee Now, and asked ordinary Americans to be a part of the cure. And the people responded.

Now the future of the country is at stake, and I'm going to ask you to get involved. This book is just the starting point of a campaign. No, I'm not running for President in 2008. But I *am* campaigning to bring back the leadership we deserve.

Won't you join me?

INDEX

ABOUT THE AUTHORS

Lee Iacocca is the former president of Ford Motor Company and Chrysler Corporation and a bestselling author. He spends his time traveling, giving speeches, and supporting the Iacocca Foundation, which funds research for a cure for diabetes.

Catherine Whitney is a writer living in New York and is the author of many books, including *Nine and Counting: The Women of the Senate*.